NEUROPSYCHOLOGY OF CRIMINAL BEHAVIOR

This book draws on findings from psychology, neurology, and genetics to offer a multi-dimensional analysis of criminal behavior. It explores the biological bases of emotions such as aggression, anger, and hostility and how they—combined with social psychological influences, such as family history and environmental conditions—may lead to violence. Specific case studies, including serial killings, mass murders, family violence, cannibalism, and hitmen, are referenced throughout, providing real-world examples of these theories in action. Issues of free will and the law are discussed, as well as suggestions for curbing violent behavior.

Feggy Ostrosky is Professor of Neuropsychology and head of the Laboratory of Neuropsychology and Psychophysiology at the National Autonomous University of Mexico. She has published 25 books, six neuropsychological tests, and over 340 journal articles and chapters in national and international peer-reviewed journals.

Alfredo Ardila is Professor of Neuropsychology at Florida International University. He earned his PhD in neuropsychology from Moscow State University. He has published widely in the fields of brain pathology, neuropsychological assessment, and cognition, and on the roles of cultural and social factors in behavior.

NEUROPSYCHOLOGY OF CRIMINAL BEHAVIOR

Feggy Ostrosky and Alfredo Ardila

WITH THE COLLABORATION OF FERNANDO DÍAZ COLORADO

Routledge
Taylor & Francis Group

NEW YORK AND LONDON

First published 2018
by Routledge
711 Third Avenue, New York, NY 10017

and by Routledge
2 Park Square, Milton Park, Abingdon, Oxon OX14 4RN

Routledge is an imprint of the Taylor & Francis Group, an Informa business

© 2018 Taylor & Francis

Library of Congress Cataloging-in-Publication Data
Names: Ostrosky, Feggy, author. | Ardila, Alfredo, author.
Title: Neuropsychology of criminal behavior / Feggy Ostrosky & Alfredo Ardila; with the collaboration of Fernando Diaz Colorado.
Description: 1 Edition. | New York : Routledge, 2018.
Identifiers: LCCN 2017016802 | ISBN 9781138092112 (hard back : alk. paper) | ISBN 9781138092129 (paper back : alk. paper) | ISBN 9781315107714 (ebook)
Subjects: LCSH: Criminology. | Criminal behavior—Psychological aspects. | Neuropsychology.
Classification: LCC HV6025. O78 2018 | DDC 364.3—dc23
LC record available at https://lccn.loc.gov/2017016802

ISBN: 978-1-138-09211-2 (hbk)
ISBN: 978-1-138-09212-9 (pbk)
ISBN: 978-1-315-10771-4 (ebk)

Typeset in Bembo
by Keystroke, Neville Lodge, Tettenhall, Wolverhampton

CONTENTS

FOREWORD

Since 1994, when I—Feggy Ostrosky, the first author—began studying the neuro-biology of violence, I have been privileged to be able to access 370 violent people and dangerous criminal offenders detained in high-security prisons in Mexico. Among these was a female serial killer who received the longest sentence in the history of criminal offenders in Mexico (756 years in prison) and is accused of killing 18 elderly women and attempting to kill two others. I have also been given access to several people who have committed multiple homicides, and kingpins and members of organized crime and drug cartels.

I study them in high-security prisons through interviews about life history, electro-physiological studies, neuroimaging, and neuropsychological and genetic testing.

As emotions are so important for moral behavior, I am interested in the question of what happens in the brains of serial killers and those who commit multiple homicides. How do they process moral stimuli? To explore the answers to these questions, we studied the brain correlates of basic and moral emotions in a group of controls and in a group of criminal offenders; brain metabolism and brain activity were recorded while the subjects were viewing fear and neutral faces, as well as pictures of emotionally charged unpleasant scenes with and without moral content, and emotionally pleasant and neutral pictures. In total, 240 color pictures were used. All the stimuli were previously standardized in our laboratory according to four categories: (1) unpleasant pictures with moral content (e.g. physical assaults, war scenes), (2) neutral pictures (e.g. house-hold objects, people), (3) unpleasant pictures without moral content (e.g. body mutilations, dangerous animals), and (4) pleasant pictures, including scenes of people and landscapes.

Antisocial behaviors can cause great suffering, ranging from minor actions, such as cheating during school examinations, to major crimes, such as stealing and killing others in cold blood. Violent behaviors are alarmingly common in our society and are considered a public health problem. What moves human beings to hurt others, including relatives and/or strangers? Can these impulses and actions be prevented or controlled? By studying violent people and their histories, my research has been aimed at understanding the causes of violent behaviors and developing preventive programs and effective treatments. Through my research, I try to answer the questions of whether or not there are critical periods for intervention and what the key issues are that preventive programs should include. Should we work with an offender's children, caregivers, and/or social group?

Currently, a pressing question in both family and social environments is how to raise honest and self-controlled children in a complex and morally ambiguous world, especially if we consider the fragile bonds that can exist between the family, the school, and the community. What factors contribute to the full development of moral integrity? Two pillars of moral behavior are fairness (which is related to justice) and empathy (i.e. compassion).

Some theories emphasize that rewarding ethical actions and punishing non-ethical acts is a useful strategy for building moral integrity. However, several studies have shown that if we discipline our children based purely on external reinforcement, namely reward or punishment, we are teaching them to avoid dishonest behaviors—such as stealing, cheating, and corruption—only when there is a probability or risk of being caught. It is necessary for our children to properly "internalize" and *feel emotionally* these values to drive and guide their behavior.

Other people advocate emphasizing the teaching of values; however, raising honest, self-disciplined, and committed individuals requires much more than just simple theoretical stories, lessons, and advice on moral values.

To prevent violence, we believe that it is important to understand what leads individuals to become violent.

At the time of writing, Alfredo Ardila, the second author, was working on the neuropsychological evaluation of homicides in Miami (Florida). A solid collaboration between the first and second authors of this book has been established, resulting in several publications (e.g. Ardila & Ostrosky-Solís, 2009; Ostrosky-Solís et al., 2008; Ostrosky-Solís & Ardila, 2010). An initial systematic analysis of the neuropsychological aspects of aggression was presented in the book *Mentes Asesinas: La Violencia en Tu Cerebro* (*Criminal Minds: The Violence in Your Brain*) written by Ostrosky (2007).

We considered that it was time to put together the available information about criminal behavior into a single book. We have included the best specific examples of the different types of criminal behavior to which we have access.

We are lucky to have collaborated with an expert in the area, Fernando Díaz Colorado. He has written a chapter about the crimes of paramilitarism in Colombia (Chapter 9). He is a teacher in the Law and Psychology departments at several Colombian universities. He is also a teacher of criminology at the Humani Institute in Leon, Guanajuato, Mexico. He has spoken nationally and internationally on subjects related to victimology, criminology, and legal psychology and is a founding member of the Asociación Latinoamericana de Psicología Jurídica y Forense (Latin American Legal and Forensic Psychology Association) and of the organization Opción Vida, Justicia y Paz (Option Life, Justice and Peace). He is also the author of half a dozen books related to the topics of psychology and criminality.

We sincerely hope that this book can contribute to advancing the understanding of criminal behavior from a psychological, neurological, and neuropsychological perspective.

Feggy Ostrosky

Alfredo Ardila

References

Ardila, A., & Ostrosky-Solís, F. (2009). Neuropsicología de los asesinos en serie [Neuropsychology of serial killers]. *Revista de Neurologia*, 48(3), 162–163.

Ostrosky, F. (2007). *Mentes Asesinas: La Violencia en Tu Cerebro* [*Criminal Minds: The Violence in Your Brain*]. Mexico City: Quinto Sol.

Ostrosky-Solís, F., & Ardila, A. (2010). Neurobiologia de la psicopatia [Neurobiology of psychopaths]. In: Munoz-Delgado, J., Moreno C., & Diaz, J.L. (eds), *Agresión y Violencia: Cerebro, Comportamiento y Bioética* [*Aggression and Violence: Brain, Behavior and Bioethics*]. Mexico City: Herder. pp. 271–287.

Ostrosky-Solís, F., Vélez-García, A., Santana-Vargas, D., Pérez, M., & Ardila, A. (2008). A middle-aged female serial killer. *Journal of Forensic Sciences,* 53(5), 1223–1230.

1

UNDERSTANDING VIOLENCE

Introduction

In spite of technological and social advances, violent behaviors continue to be common in our contemporary world. Due to the magnitude of these behaviors, they are also considered a public health problem (World Health Organization, 2002). Violent behaviors are seen at a variety of levels, from domestic abuse to mass homicide and wars. Table 1.1 shows the percentage of deaths that are the result of violence in a variety of countries around the world. Annually, there are almost one and a half million violent deaths worldwide and the vast majority of them are in low- and middle-income countries. Homicides represent almost half a million deaths annually.

However, violent deaths are unequally distributed among different countries, among different age ranges, and by gender. Homicide rates vary in different

TABLE 1.1 Global estimated violence-related deaths (homicides, suicides, and deaths related to wars) at the end of the twentieth century

	Deaths per 100,000 inhabitants	Proportion of total (%)
Homicide	8.8	31.3
Suicide	14.5	49.1
War-related	5.2	18.6
Total	**28.8**	**100.0**
Low- to middle-income countries	32.1	91.1
High-income countries	14.4	8.9

Source: Dahlberg & Krug, 2006

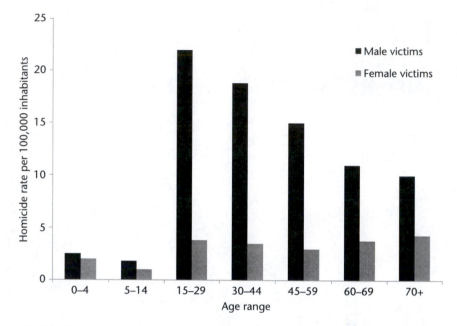

FIGURE 1.1 Distribution of homicides by gender and age range (modified and adapted from World Health Organization, 2011)

regions of the world. Statistics show that there are particularly violent regions, such as Southern Africa and different Latin American regions (Central and South America and the Caribbean). Western European countries have the lowest levels of violent deaths (UNODC, 2013).

Similarly, the age and gender distribution of violent deaths is not even (Figure 1.1). Victims of violent deaths are significantly more often male than female, particularly in the medium age ranges. In addition, violent deaths are perceptibly more common in young adults than in any other stages of life.

In some countries, homicides represent one of the leading causes of death. As mentioned, Latin American countries experience particularly high levels of violence and there are civil conflicts in many of them, which lead to perceptible increases in the number of violent deaths, such as in Colombia and Mexico.

Despite the fact that the League of Nations was initially created, followed by the United Nations, to avoid wars among nations, those efforts have been partially unsuccessful; aggression not only among people but also among nations continues to be significant. In fact, the twentieth century saw some of the worst wars that humankind has known. Table 1.2 shows the 25 wars throughout history that have resulted in more than one million deaths. Of these, 12 (almost 50%) happened in the twentieth century, showing that this century was particularly violent.

In the same way, if we consider homicides over recent decades, it is evident that (1) a significant decrease is not observed, but there is fluctuation over the years

TABLE 1.2 The most deadly wars (which resulted in more than one million deaths) in the history of humankind. Twelve of them (in bold) took place in the twentieth century (Roser, 2016)

60,000,000–85,000,000—World War II (1939–1945)

40,000,000–70,000,000—Mongol conquests (1206–1324)

36,000,000–40,000,000—Three Kingdoms War (184–280)

25,000,000—Qing Dynasty conquest of Ming Dynasty (1616–1662)

20,000,000—Taiping Rebellion (1850–1864)

20,000,000—Second Sino-Japanese War (1937–1945)

17,000,000—World War I/Great War (1914–1918)

13,000,000—An Lushan Rebellion (755–763)

7,500,000—Chinese Civil War (1927–1949)

7,000,000–20,000,000—Conquests of Tamerlane (1370–1405)

5,000,000–9,000,000—Russian Civil War and Foreign Intervention (1917–1922)

8,000,000–10,000,000—Dungan Revolt (1862–1877)

3,500,000–6,000,000—Napoleonic Wars (1803–1815)

3,000,000–11,500,000—Thirty Years' War (1618–1648)

2,500,000–5,400,000—Second Congo War/Great War of Africa (1998–2003)

2,000,000–4,000,000—French Wars of Religion (Huguenot Wars) (1562–1598)

2,000,000—Shaka's conquests (1816–1828)

1,200,000—Korean War (1950–1953)

800,000–3,800,000—Vietnam War/Second Indochina War (1955–1975)

1,000,000–2,000,000—Mexican Revolution (1910–1920)

1,000,000—Iran–Iraq War/First Persian Gulf War (1980–1988)

1,000,000—Japanese invasions of Korea (1592–1598)

1,000,000—Biafra War (1967–1970)

957,865–1,622,865—Soviet war in Afghanistan (1979–1989)

868,000–1,400,000—Seven Years' War (1756–1763)

(Figure 1.2) and (2) there are important regional differences: the homicide rate in some regions of the world is very high and in other regions is very low. Honduras is the country with the highest homicide rate, at 90.4 per 100,000 inhabitants per year. Japan has the lowest homicide rate, at 0.3 per 100,000 inhabitants per year—that is, 300 times lower than the highest rate (UNODC, 2013).

The possibility of being at any moment another victim of violence can make us live in constant fear; it can have a serious impact on our quality of life and it can become a factor that determines all of our activities: the places we go, the length of time that we stay there, the kind of security that we try to get, how we dress, what time we leave the house, and where and when we work. Undoubtedly,

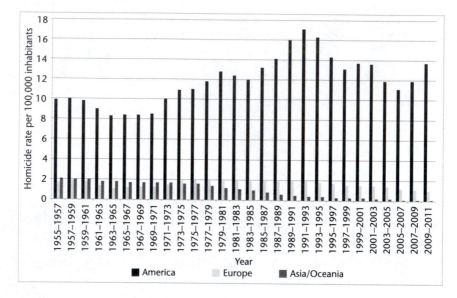

FIGURE 1.2   Homicides in different regions of the world between 1955 and 2011 (modified and adapted from UNODC, 2013)

violence, aggression, and homicide have imposed, throughout history, high costs on the quality of human life.

In an effort to combat this impact, there have been an increasing number of investigations looking at understanding the causes of violence (e.g. Geen & Donnerstein, 1998; Gilligan, 1996; Jewkes, 2002; Zimring & Hawkins, 1997) and developing, as a result, effective treatments (e.g. Brieden, Ujeyl, & Naber, 2002; Connor, 2002; Connor et al., 2006; Gerevich, Bácskai, & Czobor, 2007). Surely, in the future, the number of investigations and publications that try to better understand individual and social violence will continue to grow.

Violence and Aggression

The natural starting point in looking into this area is to understand what we mean by aggression and violence, and to determine if these are different or partially coincident phenomena (Siegel, 2005). Violence and aggression seem to be synonyms. However, it is typical in the study of these behaviors to consider that violence is different from aggression because the latter has an important biological function in the acquisition and defense of territory and food sources.

SOME DEFINITIONS

Aggression: the act of attacking someone to kill, injure, or cause harm to him or her. It has an important biological function in the acquisition and defense of territory and food sources.

Violence: behaviors or situations that cause or threaten to do harm or lead to serious subjugation. It is a kind of aggressive behavior that is exerted with the purpose of causing harm.

Homicide: a crime that consists of killing someone without the concurrence of circumstances of perfidy, cost, or aggravated brutality.

Assassination: the action and effect of killing with premeditation.

Assassinate: to kill someone with premeditation, perfidy, etc.

Crime: a serious felony; the voluntary action of killing or injuring someone seriously.

Criminal behavior: antisocial behavior that includes a wide range of acts and activities that infringe rules and social expectations. Most of them involve actions against the environment, people, and properties.

Cruelty: inhumanity, fieriness of mind, and impiety.

Hostility: a permanent state of anger.

Psychopathy: a personality disorder characterized by enduring antisocial behavior, diminished empathy and remorse, and disinhibited or bold behavior.

Sociopathy: a personality disorder characterized by antisocial behavior involving a lack of a sense of moral responsibility or social conscience.

Maltreatment: excessive cruelty.

Sadism: refined cruelty, with pleasure gained by the person who executes it.

Ire: fury or violence associated with the desire for revenge, rage, or rancor.

Anger: a movement of spirit that causes ire against somebody.

Some psychologists and psychiatrists distinguish between benign aggression and malignant aggression; the latter can be called violence. For example, Fromm (1973) defines benign aggression as a brief reaction to protect ourselves from danger. By contrast, malignant aggression is hurting others purely for sadistic pleasure. Fromm believes that people feel helplessly compelled to conform to the rules of society, to conform at work, and to be obedient to authority in all situations. This lack of freedom to make decisions and the inability to find meaning and love in one's life causes resentment and sometimes malignant and sadistic aggression.

Then, we might ask: in what way does a personality that shows malignant aggression (violence) emerge? Some people can be hostile and seem to find pleasure in causing harm, killing, or destroying. Unfortunately, multiple examples of this kind of situation can be found in daily life—for example, the man who attacks his wife or partner and demands constant attention; the mother who imposes her authority over her children and takes advantage of their weakness; and the boss who, from his or her slightly higher position of power, enjoys abusing his or her authority and humiliating his or her subordinate employees.

Ingredients of Violence

Violence is an aggressive behavior that is exerted with the intention of causing physical or psychological harm. It is important to note that the inclusion of the word "intention" is crucial, as physical and psychological harm that occurs by accident or without intention is not and must not be considered as violence. In other words, aggression can exist without violence—for example, when we defend ourselves against a physical attack or when we hit another person accidentally—but violence cannot exist without aggression, and this type of aggression is always exerted with the purpose of causing harm.

Psychological, anthropological, and biological dimensions of these two terms have been investigated (Neades & Jack, 2007). Through such investigations, it is often shown that human aggression is not innate, but learned and encouraged by culture. In particular, anthropologists say that many human societies are pacific, and such societies that are less industrialized (e.g. hunters and gatherers) show low levels of aggression and value other attributes such as compassion and solidarity (Walker, 2001).

Ethologists, namely experts in animal behavior, however, do not have the same opinions. According to Konrad Lorenz (1966), who won the Nobel Prize in Physiology and Medicine in 1973, all of us are carriers of an animal instinct that wants to manifest itself, but it is almost always repressed because of an energetic system of social control. For Lorenz, this repression is precisely what sets us free and turns us into human beings. In this system, the brain is the organ that guides our behavior and, thus, is the fundamental object that must be considered to understand the origin of behavior.

The Soul's Fragile Dwelling Place

It has been said that Shakespeare wrote: "The brain is the soul's fragile dwelling place." In his own words, the playwright suggests that a very thin line exists between mental health and sickness. Surely, all of us experience sadness and worry, but when these emotions are excessive or inappropriate in certain circumstances, we pass from normal to pathological situations. Therefore, the difference between sadness and depression, fear and phobias, happiness and mania, and aggression and violence can be extremely subtle.

From the biological point of view, emotions have been systematically studied from a neurological perspective, and in many cases they have been found to be clearly related to specific brain structures (Dalgleish, 2004; Denton, 2006; Fox, 2008; LeDoux, 1996). Consequently, it is important to remember that aggressive behavior may have its origin in multiple factors. These can be hereditary and/or learned during development, although it is usually the result of an interrelation between both types of factor.

Historically, two main theories have coexisted that purport to explain the origin of aggression. The first was initially postulated by Jean-Jacques Rousseau in the eighteenth century (Rousseau, 1762); it supposes that human beings are born fundamentally good and they become aggressive or violent during their development as a result of cultural learning. This vision is the basis of social learning theory, developed by renowned contemporary psychologists such as the American Alfred Bandura (1973, 1977). In line with this theory, a document of the National Academy of Sciences of the United States of America argues that aggressive and violent manifestations are learned behaviors related to frustration and says that learning occurs through observations of models of these behaviors (Anderson & Huesmann, 2003).

The second theory comes from thoughts of philosophers such as the Englishman Thomas Hobbes, author of the classic *Leviathan* (Hobbes, 1651), and experts in animal behavior such as the Austrian zoologist Konrad Lorenz (Lorenz, 1966; Lorenz & Leyhausen, 1973). In this theory, it is postulated that children learn not to be aggressive. We are born with selfish and aggressive tendencies and it is necessary to learn to inhibit those tendencies during development. From this perspective, aggression is understood as a self-regulating disorder that manifests as unstable behavior, which exists from birth and may have neurological origins.

However, the theories of learning to be aggressive and of learning not to be aggressive are not completely opposed. Longitudinal studies (long-term monitoring), in which aggressive and violent behaviors in children are observed from birth to adolescence, show that subgroups may exist in these types of behaviors (Dubow, Boxer, & Huesmann, 2008; Dubow, Huesmann, & Boxer, 2003; Huesmann, Dubow, & Boxer, 2009, 2011; Kokko et al., 2009). That is to say, we are born with a predisposition for aggression and later we learn in what moments we can or must express or inhibit these tendencies. So, it is possible to conclude that the biological approach emphasizes that aggression is inherent to human beings as a means of survival, but that violent behavior is the result of social learning.

Comparisons between similar countries with very different levels of violence, such as Ecuador and Colombia, can be particularly interesting. The intentional homicide rate is about three times higher in Colombia (31.9 per 100,000 inhabitants) than in Ecuador (12.4 per 100,000) (UNODC, 2013). However, the fundamental, social, and cultural conditions of these countries are quite similar; they are neighboring countries that even, during a period of time, formed a single unified country. The obvious question is: why is there such a significant difference between them? To answer this question, we must assume that there are specific cultural factors and conditions that lead to this obvious difference, although it is not easy to determine these specific cultural factors and conditions.

The comparison of the same people over time is another interesting example. For instance, the Mongol conquests represent one of the bloodiest and most violent events in human history (with about 40,000,000–70,000,000 victims); as a matter of fact, it was the second deadliest episode in human history (White, 2012). Today, the rate of intentional homicides in Mongolia is relatively low (9.7 per 100,000 inhabitants) (UNODC, 2013). What has changed in Mongolia over the last few centuries to create this enormous historical difference in violence?

From the point of view of sociobiology, aggression is considered as a behavior with adaptive purposes, which has developed through evolution (Alcock, 2001). This theory postulates that, biologically, all animal species participate in aggressive behaviors—for example, through threatening gestures or real attacks against other animals; it also says that there are biological foundations of aggressive behavior and that specific brain structures, diverse hormones, and neurotransmitters regulate such behavior. It is important to emphasize that hormones and chemical substances do not cause aggressive behavior; what these really do is reduce or increase our threshold to express aggressiveness (Adelson, 2004; O'Connor, Archer, & Wu, 2004).

Anger and Hostility

Aggression (an explicit behavior) is a response to an emotional state (an internal state). A permanent state of anger is known as hostility. It can be said that all of us know anger; it is experienced either as a temporary discomfort or as an early step towards an outburst of rage. In spite of being a common human emotion, if it gets out of our control, it may become a destructive emotion (aggression), which might cause family-related, social, and labor problems, and these can seriously affect quality of life.

Anger may occur as a response to frustration, which in turn is generated when what we wish for is not obtained or when someone or something interferes with the obtainment of a desired goal (Blair, 2010). Events that provoke frustration may be physical or psychological. The immediate way to express anger consists in an aggressive response. In fact, aggression is an adaptive response to threat; it inspires powerful feelings and behaviors that let us fight and defend ourselves when we are attacked (Lorenz, 1966). A certain amount of anger is necessary for survival, as it may increase our level of alertness and optimize defense behaviors. However, extreme and uncontrolled anger generates rage, which, in addition to being the most dangerous emotion, is probably the source of some of the main problems that threaten our society, such as war, crime, dating/domestic abuse and child abuse, bad labor conditions, and poor health status (e.g. headaches, hypertension, gastrointestinal disorders, and heart attacks).

The Manifestation of Anger

A broad range of processes can be used to express feelings of anger. It has been proposed that there are three basic forms: communication, suppression, and hostility.

1. *Communication.* This involves expressing our feelings of anger in an assertive and non-aggressive way. This is the most rational way to express anger.
2. *Suppression.* This involves hiding or suppressing anger. This has also been called passive aggression or passive–aggressive behavior (Millon et al., 2004). It can also appear by means of subtle or passive opposition; the best example of this is when a person says he or she is tired, does not respond, and acts as if he or she does not understand instructions. Victimizing is another way to express suppressed anger. In this case, a person assumes that someone or something has harmed him or her and, instead of accusing or identifying the cause of that harm, the person feels that the world is against him or her, or else that other people are trying to make him or her feel miserable. Victims feel helpless and powerless, and that is the reason why they take little responsibility for what is happening to them.
3. *Hostility.* People who pity themselves, are pessimistic, always feel sad, or are extremely jealous are probably concealing an enormous degree of hostility (Ryckman, 2012). Those who are permanently cynical and aggressive towards others and make hurtful and painful comments are those who have not yet learned to express their anger in a constructive manner; consequently, they do not have successful interpersonal relationships.

Hostility affects the physical and emotional health of those suffering it, as they are vulnerable to cardiovascular diseases. Johan Denollet, a researcher in the School of Medicine at Ghent University in Belgium, has discovered that frequent and extreme episodes of anger generate high levels of endocrine and cardiovascular responses, which contribute to the development and exacerbation of endocrine diseases and cardiovascular disturbances (Denollet et al., 1996; Strik et al., 2003). In addition, he has developed the concept of type D personality, which is not a mental disease but a set of human characteristics, the most important of which are negative emotions and social inhibition. A study of 875 people revealed that patients with type D personality were four times more likely to suffer cardiovascular attacks or die after a heart attack (Denollet, 2000).

The Road to Violence

One of the most determinant factors in the life of a child, and perhaps the most important, is the relationship with his or her parents. The bond with parents may be defined as the union between the child and the caregiver; however, this relationship may be very fragile if there is abuse towards the child (Craissati, McClurg, & Browne, 2002; Sidebotham, Golding, & ALSPAC Study Team, 2001). Being exposed to family violence clouds a child's emotions, diminishes self-esteem, and undermines his or her ability to establish attachment (Donnellan et al., 2005). An unstable and uncertain bond between the child and the caregiver is a predictor of aggression. It has been found that difficulties in attachment in childhood cause hostile-aggressive behaviors during school years.

Moreover, attachment is related to social competence (Isley et al., 1999). It is common for children to experience changes during their school years in their relationships with friends. A gradual decrease in instrumental aggression can be observed; that is, children use aggression less and less to obtain what they want. However, hostile aggression may increase in the form of verbal attacks or may be practiced by creating "gangs" and groups of friends.

Styles of Parenting

Most parents frequently deal with the problem of how to adapt their children's behavior to their own wishes of what they want them to be. Some parents establish very high standards and insist that their children strive for excellence in all areas. Other parents demand very little and seldom try to be an influence over their children's behavior. Eleanor Maccoby, Emeritus Professor in the School of Psychology at Stanford University, argues that most parents tend to adopt one of three general styles of interaction with their children (Collins et al., 2000; Maccoby & Martin, 1983). Each style is a different combination of factors, which can be grouped as follows:

1. acceptance and warmth versus rejection
2. firmness versus permissiveness
3. respect for autonomy versus control.

The multiple combinations of these characteristics of interaction that parents use send different messages to children during their development. These are in turn translated into traits, such as self-esteem, self-control, social competence, and responsibility—or, otherwise, the absence of them. Therefore, these factors ultimately mold our personality, the way in which we relate to others, and the way in which we deal with new situations.

According to a theory formulated by John Borkowski (Borkowski, Ramey, & Bristol, 2002; Borkowski, Ramey, & Stile, 2002), Professor of Psychology at the University of Notre Dame, four basic parenting styles can be observed:

1. *Authoritarian parents.* These parents are controlling, rigid, cold, and very demanding. Their word is law, their values are very strict, and they demand blind obedience from their children. They do not accept disagreement manifestations.
2. *Indulgent parents.* In contrast to authoritarian parents, these parents provide their children with inconsistent and very half-hearted feedback. They demand very little from their children, do not feel responsible for their development, and do not set behavioral limits or controls.
3. *Parents with authority.* These parents tend to be firm and set clear and consistent limits. In spite of the fact that they tend to be strict—similar to authoritarian parents—they give emotional support to their children. They try to reason with them, offer explanations about the reasons why they should behave in a certain way, and give reasons for their punishments. They encourage their children's independence.
4. *Neglectful parents.* These parents do not show interest in their children and exhibit indifferent and rejection behaviors. They show total emotional detachment and perceive that their only role is to offer shelter, food, and clothes. In extreme cases, this parenting style leads to abandonment, which could be considered a type of child abuse.

Different parenting styles will foster different personalities in children. Children of authoritarian parents tend to be withdrawn and less sociable. Girls are dependent on the parental figure while boys are hostile. Indulgent parents have children who tend to be emotionally unstable and dependent, and lack social abilities and self-control. Children of parents with authority show more adjusted personalities. They are independent, friendly, assertive, and cooperative. They exhibit high levels of achievement and are generally successful. They regulate their behavior properly, both in their interpersonal relationships and individually. The children of neglectful parents are the most affected. Their lack of emotional attachment affects emotional development and produces slightly self-involved individuals with emotional detachment, which in turn affects their physical and cognitive development.

The analysis of parenting styles is fundamental to understanding aggression, as some styles can clearly lead to the development of aggressive people and thus potential criminals.

Moral Integrity

Immanuel Kant, in *Fundamental Principles of the Metaphysic of Morals* (1797), suggested that only the person who wants to be moral is moral. A very frequent question at both a family and a social level is: how can children be educated to be honest and have self-control in a complex and morally ambiguous world where traditional ties between family, school, and community are unstable? A significant proportion of human suffering originates from those behaviors known as antisocial, which vary from minor infringements, such as cheating in games with friends, to felony crimes, such as stealing from banks or even committing cold-blooded murders.

Antonio Damasio, head of the Department of Neurology at the University of Iowa, has suggested that neuronal networks exist for pro-social behavior, which may be affected in the case of damage to the prefrontal lobes of the brain (Damasio, 1994; Damasio, Tranel, & Damasio, 1990). According to Damasio, patients who suffer damage to these areas show severe cases of antisocial behavior. In addition, it is well known that early experiences, formal education, and daily interpersonal experiences can shape the neuronal architecture of these brain areas, which are, notably, related to emotions and moral behavior (Anderson et al., 1999).

As Michael Diamond and Guy Adams (1999) pointed out, some characteristics of the fundamentals of moral behavior seem to be inherent to our species, but others need to be acquired and cultivated. Seemingly, all human beings are born with a guide, in some manner, that leads us through moral development. Several innate responses predispose us to act in an ethical way. For example, empathy—the ability to understand the experience of another person's pleasure or pain—is an innate human ability: newborns cry when they hear other newborns crying and show signs of pleasure when they hear signs of joy, such as laughing.

However, in spite of the fact that a person's emotional willingness to help may be evident, the way to help in an efficient manner must be learned and improved through social experience. To become people with moral principles, children need to not only learn to distinguish what is right from what is wrong, but also develop moral integrity to conduct themselves appropriately and behave according to their ideals. Moral development is a gradual process in which there should be consistency in the information that the child receives from their parents, from school, from the media, and from the community.

Data have been published by researchers such as Nancy Eisenberg (2004), Professor of Psychology at the University of Arizona, and Paul Rozin (Rozin, Haidt, & McCauley, 2008) from the University of Pennsylvania, regarding the factors that contribute to such moral development. In spite of the fact that, for many parents, rewarding ethical behavior and punishing non-ethical behavior is a tool used in the development of their child, the results of these studies reveal that it is necessary for the individual to "internalize" or "make values their own," so that these values guide his or her behavior. If parents only consider external contingencies (punishment or reward), dishonest behaviors such as stealing, cheating, or corruption will be avoided only when the risk of being discovered exists.

Tolerance

Competitions among political parties or between football teams may generate zeal, passion, and even radical and fundamentalist positions, which can generate uncontrolled violence (Gibson & Gouws, 2005). In 1969, for example, there was a brief war between El Salvador and Honduras, which started after a soccer game between the two countries. To understand the phenomenon of mass violence, it is necessary to analyze the concepts of tolerance and intolerance.

Tolerance is the respect for diversity: accepting and living with differences in opinion and between "parties" and regarding social, cultural, religious, gender (men and women), and achievement/performance differences. The *Merriam-Webster Dictionary* (n.d.) defines "tolerance" as "the willingness to accept feelings, habits, or beliefs that are different from your own."

Tolerance can be understood as the respect and consideration for difference and as a readiness to accept in others a way of being and behaving that is different from one's own way of being and behaving, or else as an attitude of accepting the legitimate pluralism. It is clearly a value of paramount importance in peaceful human cohabitation. By contrast, intolerance generates injustice and violence, in addition to endemic poverty and segregation.

This ability to see things from another's perspective is known, in neuropsychology, as "theory of mind" and is considered an executive function that is the origin of empathy. The theory of mind is usually defined as the ability to attribute mental states—beliefs, intents, desires, knowledge, etc.—to others and to understand that others have beliefs, desires, and intentions that are different from one's own (Leslie, Friedman, & German, 2004; Premack & Woodruff, 1978).

Control of Emotions

Erasmus (1530) said that the main hope of a nation lies in the proper education of its youth. Infancy and adolescence are evidently critical windows of opportunity to set basic emotional habits that will guide our lives and may help us to increase or decrease the probability of aggression and violence.

Psychologist Peter Salovey, from Yale University, who coined the term "emotional intelligence" (Salovey & Mayer, 1990)—which was subsequently spread by Daniel Goleman in his book *Emotional Intelligence* (1996)—described in detail a way in which intelligence can be applied to emotions:

- *Knowing our own emotions.* This is our awareness about our emotions through the recognition of a feeling while it is occurring. The inability to be aware of our own feelings leaves us exposed to them.
- *Dealing with emotions.* Dealing with feelings so that they are appropriate is an ability based on self-awareness. It includes being capable of calming down and of getting rid of excessive irritability, anxiety, and melancholy. People who lack this ability constantly fight against emotional distress, while those who are able to develop it will be able to more easily recover from adversities and problems in life.
- *Knowing our own motivation.* This involves ordering our emotions to determine our essential goal, paying attention to self-motivation and self-control, as well

as to creativity. Emotional self-control to postpone gratification and control impulses is the basis of gaining future benefits.

- *Recognizing other people's emotions.* Empathy is another ability based on emotional self-awareness. People who have empathy are more capable of reading the subtle emotional signs that indicate what other people need or want.
- *Dealing with relations.* The art of relations largely consists in knowing how to deal with other people's emotions and adapt to them.

A key ability for decreasing violence and increasing tolerance is the control of impulses. This is considered a basic executive function (Elliot, 2003; Jurado & Rosselli, 2008), which is disturbed in the case of frontal lesions, especially basal and frontal lesions. Patients with basal frontal lesions behave impulsively, are uninhibited, and are disrespectful of social regulations, as was described more than 150 years ago in the case of the patient Phineas Gage (Harlow, 1848).

As previously explained, emotional abilities such as empathy and emotional self-regulation are developed during childhood. The most important period in the process of developing mature emotional behaviors occurs during kindergarten, and feelings such as insecurity, humility, jealousy, envy, pride, and trust appear through understanding how these are experienced by others (Denham, 1998; Salovey & Sluyter, 1997). When a 5-year-old child is enrolled in the broad social world of school, social comparisons begin. These comparisons are provoked not only by extreme differences, but also by the appearance of new cognitive abilities: being able to compare ourselves with others regarding specific qualities such as popularity, attractiveness, or talent.

During the years of transition into elementary school to the end of junior high school, there are two crucial periods in a child's development. From 6 to 11 years old, school is a fundamental and defining experience that will have a strong influence on adolescence. The child's notion about his or her own value or self-esteem basically depends on his or her ability to perform appropriately at school. A child who fails at school starts to develop defensive attitudes, which may affect all aspects of life. The abilities to postpone gratification, to be socially responsible, to maintain control over one's own emotions, and to have an optimistic attitude are developed at school. The acquisition and development of executive functions are largely matched to school stages (Ardila, 2013).

Puberty, a stage of significant changes in a child's biology, intellectual abilities, and neurological performance, is also a crucial stage in a child's emotional and moral development (Shaffer & Kipp, 2013). The period from 10 to 15 years old is critical for the management of emotions and for the development of social self-esteem, through the development of confidence to establish and maintain new friends. Conversely, it is also a critical period in the appearance of antisocial behaviors; in fact, it has been often pointed out that criminal behaviors tend to manifest during adolescence (Broidy et al., 2003).

References

Adelson, R. (2004). Hormones, stress and aggression: A vicious cycle. *Monitor in Psychology*, 35(10), 18.

Alcock, J. (2001). *The Triumph of Sociobiology*. New York, NY: Oxford University Press.

Anderson, C.A., & Huesmann, L.R. (2003). Human aggression: A social-cognitive view. In: Hogg, M.A., & Cooper, J. (eds), *The Handbook of Social Psychology* (revised ed.). London: SAGE Publications. pp. 296–323.

Anderson, S.W., Bechara, A., Damasio, H., Tranel, D., & Damasio, A.R. (1999). Impairment of social and moral behavior related to early damage in human prefrontal cortex. *Nature Neuroscience*, 2(11), 1032–1037.

Ardila, A. (2013). Development of emotional and metacognitive executive functions in children. *Applied Neuropsychology: Child*, 2(2), 82–88.

Bandura, A. (1973). *Aggression: A Social Learning Analysis*. Englewood Cliffs, NJ: Prentice Hall.

Bandura, A. (1977). *Social Learning Theory*. Englewood Cliffs, NJ: Prentice Hall.

Blair, R.J.R. (2010). Psychopathy, frustration, and reactive aggression: The role of ventromedial prefrontal cortex. *British Journal of Psychology*, 101(3), 383–399.

Borkowski, J.G., Ramey, S., & Bristol, M. (eds). (2002). *Parenting and the Child's World: Influences on Intellectual, Academic, and Social Emotional Development*. Mahwah, NJ: Erlbaum.

Borkowski, J.G., Ramey, S.L., & Stile, C. (2002). Parenting research: Implications for parenting practices and public policies. In: Borkowski, J.G., Ramey, S.L., & Bristol, M. (eds), *Parenting and the Child's World: Influences on Intellectual, Academic, and Social Emotional Development*. Mahwah, NJ: Erlbaum. pp. 363–384.

Brieden, T., Ujeyl, M., & Naber, D. (2002). Psychopharmacological treatment of aggression in schizophrenic patients. *Pharmacopsychiatry*, 35(3), 83–89.

Broidy, L.M., Nagin, D.S., Tremblay, R.E., Bates, J.E., Brame, B., Dodge, K. A., ... & Vitaro, F. (2003). Developmental trajectories of childhood disruptive behaviors and adolescent delinquency: A six-site, cross-national study. *Developmental Psychology*, 39(2), 222–245.

Collins, W.A., Maccoby, E.E., Steinberg, L., Hetherington, E.M., & Bornstein, M.H. (2000). Contemporary research on parenting: The case for nature and nurture. *American Psychologist*, 55(2), 218–232.

Connor, D.F. (2002). *Aggression and Antisocial Behavior in Children and Adolescents: Research and Treatment*. New York, NY: Guilford Press.

Connor, D.F., Carlson, G.A., Chang, K.D., Daniolos, P.T., Ferziger, R., Findling, R.L., & Steiner, H. (2006). Juvenile maladaptive aggression: A review of prevention, treatment, and service configuration and a proposed research agenda. *The Journal of Clinical Psychiatry*, 67(5), 808–820.

Craissati, J., McClurg, G., & Browne, K. (2002). The parental bonding experiences of sex offenders: A comparison between child molesters and rapists. *Child Abuse & Neglect*, 26(9), 909–921.

Dahlberg, L.L., & Krug, E.G. (2006). Violence: A global public health problem. *Ciência & Saúde Coletiva*, 11(2), 1163–1178.

Dalgleish, T. (2004). The emotional brain. *Nature: Perspectives*, 5(7), 582–589.

Damasio, A.R. (1994). *Descartes' Error: Emotion, Reason, and the Human Brain*. New York, NY: Putnam.

Damasio, A.R., Tranel, D., & Damasio, H. (1990). Individuals with sociopathic behavior caused by frontal damage fail to respond autonomically to social stimuli. *Behavioral & Brain Research*, 41(2), 81–94.

Denham, S.A. (1998). *Emotional Development in Young Children*. New York, NY: Guilford Press.

Denollet, J. (2000). Type D personality: A potential risk factor refined. *Journal of Psychosomatic Research*, 49(4), 255–266.

Denollet, J., Rombouts, H., Gillebert, T.C., Brutsaert, D.L., Sys, S.U., Brutsaert, D.L., & Stroobant, N. (1996). Personality as independent predictor of long-term mortality in patients with coronary heart disease. *The Lancet*, 347(8999), 417–421.

Denton, D. (2006). *The Primordial Emotions: The Dawning of Consciousness*. Oxford, UK: Oxford University Press.

Diamond, M.A., & Adams, G.B. (1999). The psychodynamics of ethical behavior in organizations. *American Behavioral Scientist*, 43(2), 245–263.

Donnellan, M.B., Trzesniewski, K.H., Robins, R.W., Moffitt, T.E., & Caspi, A. (2005). Low self-esteem is related to aggression, antisocial behavior, and delinquency. *Psychological Science*, 16(4), 328–335.

Dubow, E.F., Boxer, P., & Huesmann, L.R. (2008). Childhood and adolescent predictors of early and middle adulthood alcohol use and problem drinking: The Columbia County Longitudinal Study. *Addiction*, 103(Suppl. 1), 36–47.

Dubow, E.F., Huesmann, L.R., & Boxer, P. (2003). Theoretical and methodological considerations in cross-generational research on parenting and child aggressive behavior. *Journal of Abnormal Child Psychology*, 31(2), 185–192.

Eisenberg, N. (2004). Prosocial and moral development in the family. In: Thorkildsen, T.A., & Walberg, H.J. (eds), *Nurturing Morality*. New York, NY: Springer. pp. 119–135.

Eliott, R. (2003). Executive functions and their disorders. *British Medical Bulletin* 65(1), 49–59.

Erasmus, D. (1530). *The Education of Children*. Public domain book (2011). Retrieved on May 4, 2017 from: https://archive.org/details/theeducationofch28338gut.

Fox, E. (2008). *Emotion Science: Cognitive and Neuroscientific Approaches to Understanding Human Emotions*. Melbourne, Australia: Palgrave MacMillan.

Fromm, E. (1973). *The Anatomy of Human Destructiveness*. New York, NY: Holt, Rinehart & Winston.

Geen, R.G., & Donnerstein, E.D. (eds). (1998). *Human Aggression: Theories, Research, and Implications for Social Policy*. San Diego, CA: Academic Press.

Gerevich, J., Bácskai, E., & Czobor, P. (2007). Aggression levels in treatment-seeking inpatients with alcohol-related problems compared to levels in the general population in Hungary. *The Journal of Nervous and Mental Disease*, 195(8), 669–672.

Gibson, J.L., & Gouws, A. (2005). *Overcoming Intolerance in South Africa: Experiments in Democratic Persuasion*. New York, NY: Cambridge University Press.

Gilligan, J. (1996). *Violence: Our Deadly Epidemic and Its Causes*. New York, NY: Putnam.

Goleman, D. (1996). *Emotional Intelligence: Why It Can Matter More than IQ*. New York, NY: Bantam Books.

Harlow, J.M. (1848). Passage of an iron rod through the head. *Boston Medical & Surgical Journal*, 39(20), 389–393.

Hobbes, T. (1651). *Leviathan: Or the Matter, Forme, and Power of a Common-Wealth Ecclesiasticall and Civill*, I. Shapiro (ed.). New Haven and London: Yale University Press (2010).

Huesmann, L.R., Dubow, E.F., & Boxer, P. (2009). Continuity of childhood, adolescent, and early adulthood aggression as predictors of adult criminality and life outcomes: Implications for the adolescent-limited and life-course-persistent models. *Aggressive Behavior*, 35(2), 136–149.

Huesmann, L.R., Dubow, E.F., & Boxer, P. (2011). The transmission of aggressiveness across generations: Biological, contextual, and social learning processes. In: Shaver, P.R., & Mikulincer, M. (eds), *Human Aggression and Violence: Causes, Manifestations, and Consequences.* Washington, DC: American Psychological Association. pp. 123–142.

Isley, S.L., O'Neil, R., Clatfelter, D., & Parke, R.D. (1999). Parent and child expressed affect and children's social competence: Modeling direct and indirect pathways. *Developmental Psychology*, 35(2), 547–560.

Jewkes, R. (2002). Intimate partner violence: Causes and prevention. *The Lancet*, 359(9315), 1423–1429.

Jurado, M.B., & Rosselli, M. (2008). The elusive nature of executive functions: A review of our current understanding. *Neuropsychology Review*, 17(3), 213–233.

Kant, I. (1797). *Fundamental Principles of the Metaphysic of Morals.* Translated and edited by Mary Gregor. Cambridge, UK: Cambridge University Press (1996).

Kokko, K., Pulkkinen, L., Huesmann, L.R., Dubow, E.F., & Boxer, P. (2009). Intensity of aggression in childhood as a predictor of different forms of adult aggression: A two-country (Finland and United States) analysis. *Journal of Research on Adolescence*, 19(1), 9–34.

LeDoux, J. (1996). Emotional networks and motor control: A fearful view. *Progress in Brain Research*, 107, 437–446.

Leslie, A.M., Friedman, O., & German, T.P. (2004). Core mechanisms in "theory of mind." *Trends in Cognitive Sciences*, 8(12), 528–533.

Lorenz, K. (1966). *On Aggression.* New York, NY: Harcourt Brace & Company.

Lorenz, K., & Leyhausen, P. (1973). *Motivation of Human and Animal Behavior: An Ethological View.* New York, NY: Van Nostrand.

Maccoby, E.E., & Martin, J.A. (1983). Socialization in the context of the family: Parent–child interaction. In: Mussen, P. (ed.), *Handbook of Child Psychology* (Vol. 4). New York, NY: Wiley.

Merriam-Webster Dictionary. (n.d.). Tolerance. Retrieved on August 2, 2017 from: www.merriam-webster.com/dictionary/tolerance.

Millon, T., Millon, C.M., Meagher, S., Grossman, S., & Ramnath, R. (2004). *Personality Disorders in Modern Life.* Hoboken, NJ: John Wiley & Sons.

Neades, B.L., & Jack, K. (2007). Violence and aggression. In: Dolan, B., & Holt, L. (eds), *Accident & Emergency: Theory into Practice.* Kent, UK: Bailliere-Tindall. pp. 205–214.

O'Connor, D.B., Archer, J., & Wu, F.C. (2004). Effects of testosterone on mood, aggression, and sexual behavior in young men: A double-blind, placebo-controlled, cross-over study. *The Journal of Clinical Endocrinology and Metabolism*, 89(6), 2837–2845.

Premack, D.G., & Woodruff, G. (1978). Does the chimpanzee have a theory of mind? *Behavioral and Brain Sciences*, 1(4), 515–526.

Roser, M. (2016). War and peace. *Our World in Data.* Retrieved on May 4, 2017 from: https://ourworldindata.org/war-and-peace/.

Rousseau, J.-J. (1762). *Du Contrat Social; ou, Principes du Droit Politique* [*The Social Contract and Other Later Political Writings*]. Cambridge, UK: Cambridge University Press (1997).

Rozin, P., Haidt, J., & McCauley, C.R. (2008). Disgust. In: Lewis, M., Haviland-Jones, J.M., & Barret, L.F. (eds), *Handbook of Emotions* (3rd edn). New York, NY: Guilford Press. pp. 757–776.

Ryckman, R.M. (2012). *Theories of Personality.* Boston, MA: Wadsworth Cengage Learning.

Salovey, P., & Mayer, J.D. (1990). Emotional intelligence. *Imagination, Cognition and Personality*, 9(3), 185–211.

Salovey, P., & Sluyter, D.J. (1997). *Emotional Development and Emotional Intelligence: Educational Implications*. New York, NY: Basic Books.

Shaffer, D.R., & Kipp, K. (2013). *Developmental Psychology: Childhood and Adolescence* (9th edn). Belmont, CA: Wadsworth Cengage Learning.

Sidebotham, P., Golding, J., & ALSPAC Study Team (2001). Child maltreatment in the "children of the nineties": A longitudinal study of parental risk factors. *Child Abuse and Neglect*, 25(9), 1177–1200.

Siegel, L. (2005). *Criminology: The Core* (2nd edn). Boston, CA: Cengage Learning.

Strik, J.J., Denollet, J., Lousberg, R., & Honig, A. (2003). Comparing symptoms of depression and anxiety as predictors of cardiac events and increased health care consumption after myocardial infarction. *Journal of the American College of Cardiology*, 42(10), 1801–1807.

UNODC (United Nations Office on Drugs and Crime) (2013). *Global Study on Homicide: Trends, Contexts, Data*. Vienna: UNODC.

Walker, P.L. (2001). A bioarchaeological perspective on the history of violence. *Annual Review of Anthropology*, 30(1), 573–596.

White, M. (2012). *Atrocities: The 100 Deadliest Episodes in Human History*. New York, NY: W.W. Norton & Company.

World Health Organization (2002). *The World Health Report 2002: Reducing Risks, Promoting Healthy Life*. Geneva: World Health Organization.

World Health Organization (2011). Causes of death 2008: Data sources and methods. Retrieved on May 3, 2017 from: www.who.int/healthinfo/global_burden_disease/cod_2008_sources_methods.pdf.

Zimring, F., & Hawkins, G. (1997). Lethal violence and the overreach of American imprisonment. In: *National Institute of Justice Research Report*. Rockville, MD: National Institute of Justice. pp. 338–358.

2

THE BRAIN AND EMOTIONS

Introduction

The study of emotions has been undertaken by a variety of professionals, including psychologists, anthropologists, and neurophysiologists. Emotions have great importance for human beings, as they are responsible for guiding and controlling our behavior. They mold our lives, as we try to maximize some of them, such as happiness, and to reduce others, such as fear. In certain situations, it seems that they control us completely, such as in "crimes of passion," in which the people involved often report that they acted "without thinking about what they were doing." In these situations, what happens in our brains?

More than 100 years ago, the English naturalist Charles Darwin postulated that emotions are impulses to act and instantaneous plans that let us face dangers, allowing us to survive (Darwin, 1872). Functionally, emotions are dispositions that prepare the organism to emit distancing and nearing behaviors; in other words, they keep us away from dangerous and unpleasant stimuli and bring us close to pleasant stimuli. Recently, this theory has been supported by scientific investigations (e.g. Damasio, 1994; LeDoux, 2001; Lindquist et al., 2012). In fact, a new discipline has appeared called "affective neuroscience," which was developed by, among others, Richard Davidson, a researcher at the University of California. This discipline has shown that all emotions, both pleasant (joy, pride, happiness, and love, among others) and unpleasant (pain, embarrassment, fear, dissatisfaction, culpability, anger, unhappiness, etc.), are deeply rooted in biology (Davidson, 2012).

The word "emotion" is derived from the Latin word *emovere*, which means "remove," "agitate," "be moved," and "arouse." The words "emotion" and "motive" have similar meanings, as both may be used to refer to arousing, sustaining, and guiding the activity of the organism. Without emotions, human beings would be little more than machines working in the same way day after day. We would not know the joys of love or the happiness of success; we would not have empathy for unhappy people or for those in pain because of the loss of a loved one; we would not know pride, envy, or jealousy. In brief, it is clear that life would be superficial and colorless, as it would lack value and meaning.

From experimental and anthropological studies conducted by a variety of researchers—such as Paul Ekman, Professor of Psychology in the Department of Psychiatry at the University of California in San Francisco (Ekman, 1992, 2007), and Paul Eslinger, Professor of Neurology at the University of Pennsylvania (Eslinger, 1998; Eslinger, Moll, & de Oliveira-Souza, 2002)—it has been proposed that there are two kinds of emotions: basic and complex or social. Basic emotions (ire, fear, happiness, sadness, surprise, and disgust) are innate and exist in all people and cultures, while complex or social emotions (culpability, pride, gratitude, compassion, and contempt, among others) are the result of social interaction and are related to the interests or well-being of societies and of people. Complex or social emotions depend on conscious evaluation and the direct influence of the social environment, and emerge from interaction with other people.

From a psychological point of view, emotions such as culpability, embarrassment, and pride are classified in the same family of auto-conscious emotions. These emotions are based on social relationships and emerge from worry and concern about other people's opinions regarding oneself or one's behavior. For example, the negative evaluation of oneself is fundamental to developing culpability and embarrassment, while the positive evaluation of "I" leads to feelings of or causes pride in oneself.

The emotional component is also fundamental in the process of rational thought. This has been shown through the fact that patients who have suffered damage to the frontal areas of the brain behave irrationally and do not measure the consequences of their actions, largely because of their inability to modulate emotions (Eslinger & Geder, 2000). In fact, this has been known since the observations of the patient Phineas Gage (Harlow, 1868).

In the same way, the emotional component is fundamental to memory processes. There is a clear connection between the brain structures that are involved in memory and those involved in emotional behavior; both are related to the limbic system (Figure 2.1). We remember what is significant—in other words, something that has emotional value (Christianson, 2014; Phelps, 2004); other situations or things do not deserve our attention and we do not store them in our memory.

In a typical person, emotions are key tools for learning and making decisions. For example, when we conduct bad business, we feel bad, and this lets us act with more caution when facing a similar situation again. In the same way, it is evident that we would not decide to whom we will get married or how we will organize our finances only on the basis of our reasoning. The emotional component is vital when we take rational decisions and it is involved at all points in our lives.

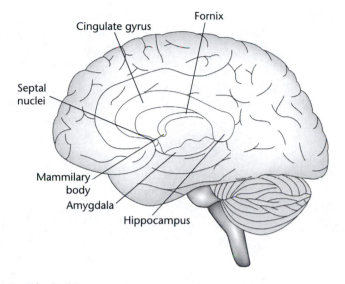

FIGURE 2.1 The limbic system

Over recent decades, research on the biological and evolutionary foundations of emotions has substantially increased (e.g. Gross, 2011; Oatley, Keltner, & Jenkins, 2006; Phillips et al., 2003). Affective neuroscience has been focused on investigating the biological foundations and processes that underlie emotions and changes in emotions. Experimental studies in this field require stimuli that, on the one hand, evoke psychological and physiological reactions in a reliable way and, on the other, can be quantitatively measured in dimensions such as valence, dominance, and the activation that the stimuli provokes.

The Emotional Brain

The limbic system is also known as the emotional brain; it contains many structures including the hypothalamus, the amygdala, the thalamus, the fornix, the hippocampus, and the anterior cingulate cortex. This system is very important because it is involved in memory and learning processes, emotional behavior, and the control of aggression (Gloor, 1997; Mega et al., 1996). This part of the brain is sufficiently complex to distinguish between and express basic emotions. However, the participation of more complex structures, in particular the prefrontal regions of the brain, is required for more subtle emotions, such as love, affection, friendship, and distrust, among others (Cardinal et al., 2002; Tranel, Bechara, & Denburg, 2002).

The amygdala is located in the temporal lobe, anterior to the hippocampus, and is one of the oldest structures of the brain. It is responsible for evaluating situations that happen in the outside world and giving an emotional meaning to environmental stimuli. However, its greatest responsibility is the management of fear, particularly fear that has been acquired through exposure to traumatic events, and such exposure can play an important role in the way in which a person expresses fear (LeDoux, 2003). As soon as the amygdala processes emotions of this kind, it causes the brain to act to enable survival—for example, by attacking another to get food or escaping from danger, perhaps from being stalked by a sexual predator. It is a structure where, in a certain manner, our emotional memory is stored.

When a stimulus that requires our attention appears, the amygdala acts to analyze its meaning, assigns an emotional sense, and in this way alerts other parts of the brain to pay attention to it. For example, if a loud noise is heard at night, it is the amygdala that sends signals to other nuclei to accelerate our pulse, triggering the sensation of fear, which puts us in a state of alertness.

Electrical stimulation of the amygdala, on the other hand, provokes a state of physiological excitation, which is translated into an accelerated pulse or increased breathing rate (Kapp, Supple, & Whalen, 1994). The ability of the amygdala to trigger the activation of the autonomic nervous system is a key element in the generation of human emotions that influence our unconscious choices.

The amygdala also acts through the stimulation of the hypothalamus (Figure 2.2), the oldest structure of the human limbic system, which is located at the upper end of the brain stem (LeDoux et al., 1988). The hypothalamus also has an internal section that is connected to the system that calms us down and an external section that is connected to the excitation of the brain. The hypothalamus can help to create basic emotions, such as ire and intense fear, as well as positive states, ranging from moderate pleasure to ecstasy. It does this by controlling the autonomic nervous system (which is responsible for modulating heart rate, blood pressure, temperature, thirst, hunger, the release of hormones, and energy production). Through the control of internal stability, the hypothalamus influences a number of emotions such as fear, displeasure, and pleasure.

The hippocampus (Figure 2.1) is another structure that is complementary to the amygdala; it helps the brain to focus on sensory stimuli and on the generation of

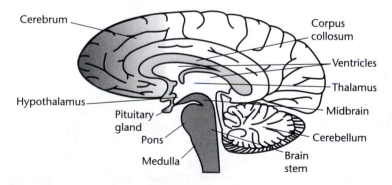

FIGURE 2.2 The hypothalamus is located below the thalamus

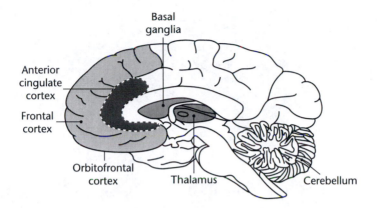

FIGURE 2.3   The location of the anterior cingulate cortex

emotions, linking these to memory, images, and learning (Anagnostaras, Gale, & Fanselow, 2001). This part of the brain is responsible for linking memories to emotions, in order to have an influence on the amygdala and the hypothalamus, and, in this way, it participates in the regulation of positive and negative emotions.

The anterior cingulate cortex (Figure 2.3) is located near the medial prefrontal cortex; in addition to being involved in behavioral initiation, it participates in emotional self-control, conflict resolution, and the recognition of mistakes (Bush, Luu, & Posner, 2000). The anterior cingulate cortex regulates the effects of intense emotional reactions through the modulation of the firing of cells of the amygdala. This structure seems to make the pacific resolution of conflicts possible, a basic principle of human socialization. The anterior cingulate cortex has important connections with the prefrontal cortex and is part of what has sometimes been called the "rational brain," which is involved in metacognitive executive functions (Ardila, 2008; Goldberg, 2009).

The emotional brain (the limbic system) is found in an old part (the allocortex) of the nervous system. The allocortex has only three or four layers of neural structures, unlike the neocortex, which has six layers. The emotional brain has structures that were developed very early in evolution, hence why emotions are more primitive than our cognitive skills; our ability to plan, analyze, and solve problems stems from the executive areas of the brain. These structural centers of the brain are located in the frontal lobes and evolved during the most recent period of the history of our species; therefore, these are the last to mature in the individual during social development (Ardila, 2008).

The Rational Brain

The cerebral cortex is the external layer of the hemispheres of the brain and constitutes approximately 77% of the volume of the human brain (Swanson, 1995).

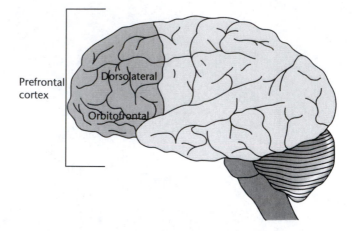

FIGURE 2.4   The prefrontal cortex, which can be divided into the dorsolateral, orbitofrontal, and medial areas (the latter is an internal section, which is not observed in the figure)

In the least developed mammals, such as rats, dogs, and non-human primates, the cortex constitutes smaller percentages of the whole brain; this depends on the species' evolutionary level. By contrast, the diencephalon (where the limbic system is partially located) makes up only 4% of the total cerebral volume. In the anterior part of the cerebral cortex are the frontal lobes, some of the most fundamental regions of the human brain. Each frontal lobe constitutes 37% of the volume of each cerebral hemisphere in humans (Semendeferi et al., 1997).

The majority of research on aggression and violence has been focused on the anterior parts of the brain, which include the frontal and temporal lobes. Through this research, the crucial role that the cerebral prefrontal areas play in controlling and monitoring emotions has been discovered (Figure 2.4). The prefrontal region of the brain is involved in what are known as "executive functions," namely the capacity for abstract thought, "intelligence," planning, the inhibition of inappropriate behaviors, and the regulation of emotions—in other words, in two basic aspects of human activity: the control of cognitive activity (metacognitive executive functions, in the dorsolateral area) and emotional control (motivational/emotional executive functions, in the orbitofrontal area) (Ardila, 2008, 2013). Motivational/emotional executive functions are of crucial importance to understanding criminal behavior.

The importance of the prefrontal cortex in intellectual functions and in social behavior can be appreciated by comparing the percentage of the frontal lobe that this cortex constitutes in different animals. The prefrontal cortex constitutes about 80% of the frontal lobes in humans, but only 55% in chimpanzees and 40%–50% in monkeys (Elston et al., 2006). The prefrontal cortex is usually subdivided into the medial cortex, the dorsolateral cortex, and the orbitofrontal cortex; it has been shown that alterations in the orbitofrontal cortex produce antisocial and violent behaviors (e.g. Antonucci et al., 2006; Blair, 2001). Therefore, the prefrontal cortex can be considered the area or the center of our self-awareness, and its development has allowed humanity to build civilizations that generate art, science, culture, and social institutions.

The prefrontal cortex is extensively connected with the rest of the brain (Barbas, 2000). It is connected to the parietal, temporal, and occipital lobes, but also to subcortical regions, including, clearly, the limbic system. Its connection to the limbic system helps to modulate and control emotional behaviors. As a matter of fact, the ventromedial areas of the prefrontal cortex are involved in the expression and control of emotional and instinctual behaviors (Fuster, 1997, 2002). This function is related to the so-called "inhibitory control" of behavior (Miller & Wang, 2006). Clinical evidence (e.g. Luria, 1969; Stuss & Knight, 2002) and experimental research (e.g. Leung & Cai, 2007; Medalla et al., 2007) suggest that the neural substrate for this inhibitory function resides mainly in the medial and orbital portions of the prefrontal cortex. Fuster (2002) points out that "The apparent physiological objective of inhibitory influences from the orbitomedial cortex is the suppression of internal and external inputs that can interfere with whatever structure of behavior, speech, or cognition is about to be undertaken or currently underway" (p. 382).

New Lie Detectors

Understanding how our brains process data and how this is affected by our emotions has helped to develop lie detection techniques, which have been used on occasion in criminological investigations. However, the utility and reliability of such techniques have caused controversy (Iacono, 2001; Iacono & Lykken, 1997; Lewis & Cuppari, 2009).

Contrary to what the majority of people suppose, lie detection is a process of supreme complexity. People must be very sensitive for lies to be detected and often we erroneously consider certain behaviors as indicators of lying. For example, it is a popular belief that a person who lies doesn't make direct eye contact. Throughout history, a variety of techniques and devices have been developed to determine if someone is telling the truth or lying. The aim of such instruments, known as "lie detectors," is to measure the physiological reactions of a person who makes a conscious decision to lie.

The origin of these devices can, perhaps, be determined through anthropological observations. For example, it is said that, in the past in China, people who were suspected of a murder used to be put to a test known as "spit rice." The mouth of the accused person was filled with dry rice and it was supposed that, if the person was guilty, he or she would be nervous and it would affect his or her generation of saliva in such a way that he or she would not be able to spit the rice out. The first device designed to detect lies was developed in 1915 and was based on the measurement of blood pressure. Over time, other variables have been added and current devices now let us measure several physiological responses simultaneously, including breathing, blood pressure, and galvanic skin response, the latter relating to the sweating of hands.

Because these devices measure and record graphically several responses at the same time, they are called "polygraphs." The principle on which these devices are based is that the discordance between explicit responses and internal thoughts causes variations in some physiological responses. Measurements of this dissonance are assessed through a variety of tests. The earliest of these tests consisted in the formulation of ten questions. Over time, the questionnaire was made more complex, involving a collection of questions that had obvious answers and of "tricky" questions; in this manner, technicians could determine if people were telling the truth or not. Nowadays, carrying out a polygraph test involves asking various questions: some where the investigator and the interviewee know the answer, such as "Is today Monday?"; some known as "control" questions, which are not related to the main topic of questioning but are used to determine how the interviewee reacts in the situation, namely when being accused of lying; and, finally, a series of questions on the topic about which the person is accused of lying.

The problem with these measurements is that some people do not feel any guilt (emotion) when they lie and so their records remain impassive, while other people, who could be "innocent," are very nervous because they are being inter-rogated and their records classify them as "guilty." In spite of their flaws, these instruments have been used for a long time in police investigations in some coun-tries, and are also now being used by some companies that need to choose people who work with confidential information.

Nowadays, much more sensitive technologies have been developed (Wolpe, Foster, & Langleben, 2005). These try to find out directly where ideas are gener-ated in the brain itself, and in this way they avoid dealing with the conscious process of lying. For example, a band with sensors that is placed around the fore-head has been used to detect changes in brain metabolism. These sensors detect changes in the prefrontal cortex, which is the area related to decision making, and, in this way, the moment when people make the decision to lie can be detected. Its advantage is that the covert activity of the prefrontal cortex is detected before the subject performs a verbal report.

Another technique is known as "thermal imaging," in which a band around the eyes detects any increases in the blood flow in this area (Dery, 2003). Investigations by the New York University School of Medicine have reported that, when people lie, more heat is absorbed around the eyes.

An important experiment was carried out using functional magnetic resonance imaging (fMRI). In this study, Daniel Langleben, a psychologist at the University of Pennsylvania, showed playing cards to 18 volunteers. Subsequently, he showed images of specific cards on a computer and asked the volunteers if they had these cards. When the subjects lied, an increase in brain metabolism was detected in the anterior cingulate cortex and in the upper part of the prefrontal cortex (Langleben et al., 2002). As mentioned previously, the anterior cingulate cortex is involved in emotions, decision making, and the resolution of conflicts. This area was intensely activated when the subjects lied.

Another innovative technique known as "brain fingerprinting" (Iacono, 2008; Rosenfeld, 2005) involves a helmet or cap with electrodes and uses electroencephalography (EEG). Words, phrases, and drawings are shown to the person wearing the cap and, in the same way as in a polygraph, the suspect is questioned about the information that he or she knows. When the subject lies, a positive wave P300 is generated after 300 milliseconds.

Methods of lie detection have been heavily criticized from the moment of their invention. However, in the topic that we are talking about, such methods can be an excellent example of strategies for the measurement of emotions. Although the advantages and disadvantages of each technique discussed above need to be determined in more detail, their utilization in the future will undoubtedly lead to important modifications in how we impart justice.

References

Anagnostaras, S.G., Gale, G.D., & Fanselow, M.S. (2001). Hippocampus and contextual fear conditioning: Recent controversies and advances. *Hippocampus*, 11(1), 8–17.

Antonucci, A.S., Gansler, D.A., Tan, S., Bhadelia, R., Patz, S., & Fulwiler, C. (2006). Orbitofrontal correlates of aggression and impulsivity in psychiatric patients. *Psychiatry Research: Neuroimaging*, 147(2), 213–220.

Ardila, A. (2008). On the evolutionary origins of executive functions. *Brain and Cognition*, 68(1), 92–99.

Ardila, A. (2013). There are two different dysexecutive syndromes. *Journal of Neurological Disorders*, 1(1), 1–4.

Barbas, H. (2000). Connections underlying the synthesis of cognition, memory, and emotion in primate prefrontal cortices. *Brain Research Bulletin*, 52(5), 319–330.

Blair, R.J.R. (2001). Neurocognitive models of aggression, the antisocial personality disorders, and psychopathy. *Journal of Neurology, Neurosurgery & Psychiatry*, 71(6), 727–731.

Bush, G., Luu, P., & Posner, M.I. (2000). Cognitive and emotional influences in anterior cingulate cortex. *Trends in Cognitive Sciences*, 4(6), 215–222.

Cardinal, R.N., Parkinson, J.A., Hall, J., & Everitt, B.J. (2002). Emotion and motivation: The role of the amygdala, ventral striatum, and prefrontal cortex. *Neuroscience & Biobehavioral Reviews*, 26(3), 321–352.

Christianson, S.A. (ed.). (2014). *The Handbook of Emotion and Memory: Research and Theory*. New York, NY: Psychology Press.

Damasio, A.R. (1994). *Descartes' Error: Emotion, Reason and the Human Brain*. New York, NY: Grosset/Putnam.

Darwin, C. (1872). *The Expression of the Emotions in Man and Animals*. London: HarperCollins (1998).

Davidson, R. (2012). *The Emotional Life of Your Brain*. London: Penguin.

Dery, G.M. (2003). Lying eyes: Constitutional implications of new thermal imaging lie detection technology. *American Journal of Criminal Law*, 31(2), 217–250.

Ekman, P. (1992). An argument for basic emotions. *Cognition & Emotion*, 6(3–4), 169–200.

Ekman, P. (2007). *Emotions Revealed: Recognizing Faces and Feelings to Improve Communication and Emotional Life*. New York, NY: Macmillan.

Elston, G.N., Benavides-Piccione, R., Elston, A., Zietsch, B., Defelipe, J., Manger, P., & Kaas, J.H. (2006). Specializations of the granular prefrontal cortex of primates: Implications for cognitive processing. *The Anatomical Record Part A: Discoveries in Molecular, Cellular, and Evolutionary Biology*, 288(1), 26–35.

Eslinger, P.J. (1998). Neurological and neuropsychological bases of empathy. *European Neurology*, 39(4), 193–199.

Eslinger, P.J., & Geder, L. (2000). Behavioral and emotional changes after focal frontal lobe damage. In: Bogousslavsky, J., & Cummings, J.L. (eds), *Behavior and Mood Disorders in Focal Brain Lesions*. Cambridge, UK: Cambridge University Press. pp. 217–260.

Eslinger, P.J., Moll, J., & de Oliveira-Souza, R. (2002). Emotional and cognitive processing in empathy and moral behavior. *Behavioral and Brain Sciences*, 25(1), 34–35.

Fuster, J.M. (1997). *The Prefrontal Cortex: Anatomy, Physiology, and Neuropsychology of the Frontal Lobe*. Philadelphia, PA: Lippincott-Raven.

Fuster, J.M. (2002). Frontal lobe and cognitive development. *Journal of Neurocytology*, 31(3–5), 373–385.

Gloor, P. (1997). *The Temporal Lobe and Limbic System*. New York, NY: Oxford University Press.

Goldberg, E. (2009). *The New Executive Brain: Frontal Lobes in a Complex World*. New York, NY: Oxford University Press.

Gross, J.J. (ed.). (2011). *Handbook of Emotion Regulation*. New York, NY: Guilford Press.

Harlow, J.M. (1868). Recovery from the passage of an iron bar through the head. *Massachusetts Medical Society Publications*, 2, 327–346.

Iacono, W.G. (2001). Forensic "lie detection": Procedures without scientific basis. *Journal of Forensic Psychology Practice*, 1(1), 75–86.

Iacono, W.G. (2008). The forensic application of "brain fingerprinting": Why scientists should encourage the use of P300 memory detection methods. *The American Journal of Bioethics*, 8(1), 30–32.

Iacono, W.G., & Lykken, D.T. (1997). The validity of the lie detector: Two surveys of scientific opinion. *Journal of Applied Psychology*, 82(3), 426–433.

Kapp, B.S., Supple, W.F., & Whalen, P.J. (1994). Effects of electrical stimulation of the amygdaloid central nucleus on neocortical arousal in the rabbit. *Behavioral Neuroscience*, 108(1), 453–460.

Langleben, D.D., Schroeder, L., Maldjian, J.A., Gur, R.C., McDonald, S., Ragland, J.D., ... & Childress, A.R. (2002). Brain activity during simulated deception: An event-related functional magnetic resonance study. *Neuroimage*, 15(3), 727–732.

LeDoux, J.E. (2001). Emotion circuits in the brain. In: Hyman, S. (ed.), *The Science of Mental Health: Fear and Anxiety*. New York, NY: Routledge. pp. 259–275.

LeDoux, J.E. (2003). The emotional brain, fear, and the amygdala. *Cellular and Molecular Neurobiology*, 23(4–5), 727–738.

LeDoux, J.E., Iwata, J., Cicchetti, P.R.D.J., & Reis, D.J. (1988). Different projections of the central amygdaloid nucleus mediate autonomic and behavioral correlates of conditioned fear. *The Journal of Neuroscience*, 8(7), 2517–2529.

Leung, H.C., & Cai, W. (2007). Common and differential ventrolateral prefrontal activity during inhibition of hand and eye movements. *The Journal of Neuroscience*, 27(37), 9893–9900.

Lewis, J.A., & Cuppari, M. (2009). The polygraph: The truth lies within. *Journal of Psychiatry and Law*, 37(1), 85–92.

Lindquist, K.A., Wager, T.D., Kober, H., Bliss-Moreau, E., & Barrett, L.F. (2012). The brain basis of emotion: A meta-analytic review. *Behavioral and Brain Sciences*, 35(3), 121–143.

Luria, A.R. (1969). Frontal lobe syndromes. In: Vinken, P.J., & Bruyn G.W. (eds), *Handbook of Clinical Neurology* (Vol. 2). Amsterdam: North-Holland Publishing Company. pp. 725–757.

Medalla, M., Lera, P., Feinberg, M., & Barbas, H. (2007). Specificity in inhibitory systems associated with prefrontal pathways to temporal cortex in primates. *Cerebral Cortex*, 17(Suppl. 1), i136–i150.

Mega, M.S., Cummings, J.L., Salloway, S., & Malloy, P. (1996). The limbic system: An anatomic, phylogenetic, and clinical perspective. *The Journal of Neuropsychiatry and Clinical Neurosciences*, 9(3), 315–330.

Miller, P., & Wang, X.J. (2006). Inhibitory control by an integral feedback signal in prefrontal cortex: A model of discrimination between sequential stimuli. *Proceedings of the National Academy of Sciences of the United States of America*, 103(1), 201–206.

Oatley, K., Keltner, D., & Jenkins, J.M. (2006). *Understanding Emotions*. Malden, MA: Blackwell Publishing.

Phelps, E.A. (2004). Human emotion and memory: Interactions of the amygdala and hippocampal complex. *Current Opinion in Neurobiology*, 14(2), 198–202.

Phillips, M.L., Drevets, W.C., Rauch, S.L., & Lane, R. (2003). Neurobiology of emotion perception I: The neural basis of normal emotion perception. *Biological Psychiatry*, 54(5), 504–514.

Rosenfeld, J.P. (2005). Brain fingerprinting: A critical analysis. *Scientific Review of Mental Health Practice*, 4(1), 20–37.

Semendeferi, K., Damasio, H., Frank, R., & Van Hoesen, G.W. (1997). The evolution of the frontal lobes: A volumetric analysis based on three-dimensional reconstructions of magnetic resonance scans of human and ape brains. *Journal of Human Evolution*, 32(4), 375–388.

Stuss, D.T., & Knight, R.T. (2002). *Principles of Frontal Lobe Function*. New York, NY: Oxford University Press.

Swanson, L.W. (1995). Mapping the human brain: Past, present, and future. *Trends in Neurosciences*, 18(11), 471–474.

Tranel, D., Bechara, A., & Denburg, N.L. (2002). Asymmetric functional roles of right and left ventromedial prefrontal cortices in social conduct, decision-making, and emotional processing. *Cortex*, 38(4), 589–612.

Wolpe, P.R., Foster, K.R., & Langleben, D.D. (2005). Emerging neurotechnologies for lie-detection: Promises and perils. *The American Journal of Bioethics*, 5(2), 39–49.

3

THE ORIGINS OF VIOLENCE

Introduction

There are many theories that try to explain the causes of violence (e.g. Ferguson & Beaver, 2009; Rapoport, 1994; Staub, 1989, 1999; Wrangham & Peterson, 1996). In fact, violence is a complex phenomenon with multiple causes, and the problem that these theories usually have is the great number of variables that have to be considered. The phenomenon of violence has been investigated and tackled from a variety of perspectives to understand it in an integral way, with psychological, neurological, and genetic factors studied in conjunction with social and cultural variables. To carry out this kind of investigation, it is important to take into account how genetic factors interact with environmental ones and the way in which these generate the conditions that lead to violence and criminogenic situations.

Biological problems, such as poor care during pregnancy—where the mother consumes alcohol and drugs—and a poorly attended childbirth, in conjunction with later maternal abandonment, are factors that could be possible causes of the development of violence in individuals.

Unfortunately, the distinction between and separation of different factors are not always easy. For example, if the individual has a low intelligence quotient, this could be considered a biological, psychological, or social factor in a study of violence. In other words, factors that contribute to violence could be categorized along a gradient for each of the possible factors: biological, psychological, and social. This would allow the possible interactions between the different variables to always be considered.

Primary Violence Versus Secondary Violence

In Chapter 1, it was noted that violence is an aggressive behavior that is exerted with the intention of causing harm (physical or psychological). In this definition, the word "intention" is crucial. Physical or psychological harm that occurs by accident and in the absence of intention is not violence. Aggression can exist without violence (e.g. when we defend ourselves against a physical attack), but violence cannot exist without aggression.

Moreover, it has been proposed that there exists "benign aggression" (Fromm, 1973), namely a brief reaction to protect ourselves from danger. By contrast, we can talk about "malignant aggression," which involves a desire to cause harm to other people. Violence can also be *primary* or *secondary*. We talk about secondary violence when it is a consequence of other conditions. In other words, some people behave violently as a consequence of other conditions, such as depression, drug and alcohol abuse, having suffered severe blows to the head, psychiatric disorders (schizophrenia, paranoid disorders, etc.), or personality disorders (e.g. so-called borderline personality). In addition to this, a variety of daily factors could worsen violence, ranging from sleep deprivation and the use of stimulants (including coffee) to excessive heat and frustrations of daily life, among others. Determining the relationship between violence and the factors that precipitate it could help in its prevention and treatment.

The basic premise is that, in the case of secondary violence, the original causes have to be treated to be able to control it. Initially, we will analyze the causes of secondary violence; later, some references to the origins of primary violence will be introduced.

Secondary Violence

The following are two factors that can lead to the appearance of secondary violence:

- *Depression and anger attacks.* Depression is related to irritability. Between 38% and 44% of depressed people experience anger attacks and report symptoms of autonomic activity associated with these attacks, such as tachycardia, hot flashes, and sweating, among others (Fava & Rosenbaum, 1999). More than 90% of individuals with depression who experience anger attacks report guilt or regret after the attacks. Regarding the kind of violence, 60% report that they attack other people physically or verbally and 30% report that they destroy or throw objects.

  Emil Coccaro, Director of the Department of Neurosciences in the School of Medicine of Philadelphia, has discovered that serotonin deficiencies are related to increases in depression and aggression. Treatment with medicines that regulate the secretion of this substance can improve depression and decrease aggressive attacks (Coccaro et al., 1997).

- *Consumption of toxic substances.* Intoxication with different substances is associated with violent behaviors (Anderson & Bokor, 2012). Between 40% and 80% of cases that are attended in emergency rooms of hospitals are related to the use of drugs or to the abuse of alcohol. The consumption of drugs is also related to domestic violence, propagating a vicious circle, as the children who grow up in this atmosphere and are witnesses of the abuse will potentially become violent adults and drug users (Cechova-Vayleux et al., 2013).

    Furthermore, alcohol decreases the levels of synthesis of serotonin and this increases the irritability of the individual and his or her aggressiveness (Komarekova & Janik, 2012). In addition to this, alcohol increases the incidence of blows to the head, which can cause changes in personality (Lin et al., 2014). In a study that was conducted by our laboratory on patients who have suffered cerebral contusions, we found that 30% of the injured people showed irritability, anxiety, fatigue, and excessive sensitivity of stimuli, especially with regard to noise, as a consequence of the injury.

    Delinquent behaviors can also be related to the consumption of psychoactive substances (Kirschbaum et al., 2013). When a person is addicted to a substance, his or her behavior is altered, and it usually leads to a decrease in his or her ability to control actions. Without considering the long-term consequences of the consumption of drugs, such as the psychopathological effects that can result from an addictive disorder, addiction can lead to cognitive impairment, depression, and changes of personality, which are enough in themselves to generate delinquent behaviors (Ardila, Rosselli, & Strumwasser, 1991; Rosselli & Ardila, 1996).

Drugs and Crime

The connection between addictive consumption and delinquent behavior can be analyzed at four different levels: abuse, intoxication, withdrawal, and dependence. Drug abuse is associated with continuous failures in the completion of daily activities—professional, domestic, or others; omission errors and serious negligence are typically observed.

Intoxication has some specific clinical manifestations; depending on the specific substance, these clinical manifestations can be observed at the psychological level and also in the activity of the nervous system. This would be the case for stimulants such as amphetamines or cocaine, namely substances that produce a sensation of increased energy, and that in high doses can cause states of extreme excitation. In the same way, the consumption of drugs such as morphine, heroin, or ecstasy can cause combined euphoric and depressive effects and changes in sensory perception.

In relation to withdrawal, the issues or specific symptoms caused by the cessation of or a decrease in the consumption of the substance involve impairment in areas of operation, and lead to a general discomfort at the physical and psychological levels, which can in turn lead to uncontrolled actions. There is no guarantee that strategies to control the withdrawal process will reduce or eliminate the possible unpleasant effects associated with withdrawal.

In dependency, there is an element of psychological and biological dependency, which involves an unstoppable desire in the consumer to obtain the substance at all costs, and to resort frequently to strategies of an antisocial kind to get it.

Thanks to technological advances, it has been possible to show that consuming a certain group of psychoactive substances is directly connected with cerebral changes. In particular, positron emission tomography (PET) has been shown to be useful in detecting the neural damage that is caused by the consumption of methylenedioxymethamphetamine (MDMA). This drug, more commonly known as ecstasy, affects the serotonin-producing neurons, which are widely connected with depression, aggression, and antisocial personality disorder. A group of scientists at the Johns Hopkins University in Baltimore used PET to study changes in the cerebral metabolism of people who "used ecstasy": 23 MDMA users in withdrawal and 19 non-MDMA controls underwent quantitative PET studies using serotonin transporter (SERT) ligands. Global and regional distribution volumes and two additional SERT-binding parameters were compared in the two subject populations using parametric statistical analyses. Global SERT reductions were found in MDMA users with both PET ligands. These quantitative PET data provide strong evidence of reduced SERT density in some recreational MDMA users (McCann et al., 2005). The loss of serotonin happens naturally as we age; however, the additional decrease that is caused by the consumption of ecstasy—which also occurs in a sporadic way—can be responsible, in the long term, for the appearance of neurological pathologies. These drugs can make paranoid symptoms worse and can lead to crimes being committed by addicts because they believe, for example, that they are defending themselves against imaginary demons.

It is important here to note that, before starting a treatment for drug addiction, it is necessary to assess if the person has other psychiatric issues. In some cases, post-traumatic stress or bipolar disorders are related to the abuse of substances (Chilcoat & Breslau, 1998) and it is possible that the proper treatment of these disorders will improve the control of aggression and decrease the consumption of narcotics. It has been suggested that the medicines that stabilize mood, such as carbamazepine and valproate, can be useful in the treatment of symptoms related to withdrawal and, in addition, can decrease impulsiveness and aggression (Leggio, Kenna, & Swift, 2008).

Types of Personality and Aggressive Behavior

The personality, our individual character, is comprised of emotional and behavioral features that are relatively stable and predictable, and that are characteristic of a person throughout his or her life. These features and behaviors determine the manner in which we interact with other people and face new situations (Larsen & Buss, 2008).

The American Psychiatric Association (1994, 2013) has identified a variety of disorders of personality associated with violence:

- *paranoid type:* a pattern of distrust and suspicion that results in the intentions of other people being interpreted maliciously;
- *schizoid type:* a pattern of a lack of connection in social relationships and restriction of emotional expression;
- *schizotypal type:* a pattern of intense discomfort in personal relationships, perceptive or cognitive distortions, and behavioral eccentricities;
- *antisocial type:* a pattern of contempt and the violation of rights of other people;
- *histrionic type:* a pattern of an excessive emotive nature and demand for attention;
- *narcissistic type:* a pattern of grandiosity, a need to be admired, and a lack of empathy.

Other identified disorders are *avoidant personality disorder*, a pattern of social inhibition, feelings of incompetence, and hypersensitivity to negative assessment; *dependent personality disorder*, a pattern of submissive and "sticky" behavior related to an excessive need to be careful; and *obsessive–compulsive personality disorder*, which is characterized by a constant worry because of order, perfectionism, and control. Within this mosaic of personality disorders, we are particularly interested in two patterns of behavior because of the direct association they could have with violent acts. In the following sections, we talk about *borderline personality* and *antisocial personality*.

Borderline Personality

This is one of the most surprising psychiatric conditions. Those with borderline personality see other individuals in white or black; they often set a person on a pedestal and then consider him or her as the worst of human beings. People who suffer from this disorder are also predisposed to explosions of aggression and transitive periods of paranoia or psychosis. They usually have a history of intense and unstable relationships. They feel empty or insecure of their identity, often experience impulses of self-destruction, and try to escape from reality through substance abuse (American Psychiatric Association, 2001).

In borderline personality, the key symptom is falsification (Hawkins et al., 2014). Those with this disorder do not have a stable identity and have a contradictory vision of themselves that they change frequently. They display changes in their reasoning when they are in situations with little structure, and can experience a temporary loss of their ability to examine or face reality. The features of this personality disorder are pathological lies, distortions of reality in conjunction with a lack of control of impulses, and primitive defense mechanisms such as negation (not accepting aspects of our life or events that happen to us). In addition, those with this disorder often display a dichotomy between the idealization and devaluation of those people who are around them.

An Example: The Case of Diego Santoy

In the early hours of March 2, 2006, Diego Santoy (a student in the Faculty of Engineering of the Autonomous University of Nuevo León in Monterrey, Mexico) entered the house of his ex-girlfriend, Erika Peña, who was 19 years old, to kill by strangulation and stabbing her siblings: Erik Azur, who was 7 years old, and María Fernanda, who was 3 years old. He was not content with these killings and decided to attack his ex-girlfriend by hitting and stabbing her, leaving her semi-conscious. He kidnapped a female domestic worker (Catalina Bautista) and escaped in Erika's car. Santoy tried to escape to Guatemala with his brother, but he was arrested in the bus station of Oaxaca on March 7, beginning a long legal process. The profile of the attacked family (the mother of the murdered children worked as a presenter on television in Monterrey) meant that the case got immediate coverage, with debates on internet forums and in local media, with disputes between people who defended Santoy and believed him to be innocent and people who wished to see him behind bars.

Santoy (who was held from March 19, 2006, in the prison of Topochico and transferred in April 2006 to the prison of Cadereyta) has been analyzed by authorities since his arrest, with interesting results. According to psychological studies, he does not show poor contact with reality. He does not report hallucinations or delirium. However, he is reported as displaying a failure to adapt himself to social rules, dishonesty indicated by his repeated lying, abrupt and non-modulated behavior, persistent irresponsibility, and a lack of remorse seen in his indifference and justification for having harmed, maltreated, or stolen from other people. A psychological study concludes that Santoy is a patient with a personality disorder. He does not show clinical signs of any mental illness such as schizophrenia or bipolar disorder in the mania phase, or of any other psychotic disorder, but, due to his inability to experience guilt, he is a very dangerous person, and has the potential to commit serious offenses.

As regards his motives to commit the murders and the kidnapping, at the beginning of the legal process, Santoy admitted his guilt but did not give a motive—a position to which he has adhered, as of the time of writing. The defense argued that Santoy was not the only implicated person and suggested that he had had a relationship with the victims' mother—a version of events that, obviously, complicated the case even more and made its resolution even more difficult.

On the other hand, the judicial process and the evidence that was given by the office of the district attorney seemed to point to the ending of the relationship between Erika and Santoy as having motivated his craving for violent revenge, resulting in the attack on his ex-girlfriend and the homicide of her siblings.

From a psychiatric perspective, Santoy meets the criteria for borderline personality. People who have this disorder have what is known as a paradoxical experience of control. In other words, they often feel that they need to be controlled by other people, to take away self-control to try to make their own reality more predictable and manageable; they also often choose a lifestyle where they are subjected to an authority (military, cults, sects, etc.) or align themselves with abusive people who exert control over them through fear. On the other hand, they can also feel the need to control other people and often accuse others of wanting to exert control over them. In addition, they show what is defined as a special interpersonal sensitivity: some have an amazing ability to "read" other people and to discover their weak points.

The key symptom of Santoy in this case is falsification: he does not have a stable identity and has a contradictory vision of himself. First, he declared that he was guilty of the murders, but then he argued that everything was planned by Erika, his ex-girlfriend. He is, clearly, a pathological liar. The way in which he carried out the homicides also shows a distortion of his reality, in conjunction with a lack of control of his impulses; he also showed primitive defense mechanisms such as negation and a dichotomy between the idealization and devaluation of those people who were around him. Seemingly, one of his characteristics that triggered this murder was pathological jealously.

Everything seems to point to the fact that Santoy lives in a state of permanent emotional instability, a "rollercoaster" existence that is demonstrated by the up-and-down relationship that he had with Erika. People with this disorder live constantly in extremes and are very sensitive to negative emotional stimuli.

Borderline personalities often pass easily from euphoria to depression, from ingenuous credulity to paranoid distrust, and from love to hatred. All of this is a consequence of a mentality that does not let the person deal, psychologically, with variations, adjustments, or mixed feelings. It is everything or nothing. This is why he may have decided that Erika belonged to him and not to somebody else. It is possible that this personal dynamic is what led him to commit the crime, with his intention being to demonstrate his power to his ex-girlfriend. It may have been a desperate search for his lost identity as a result of the relationship breaking up.

In addition to the dramatic nature of the case and its tragic ending, it has caused surprise among and had an impact on all of the people involved because of a series of inconsistencies that emerged through the judicial proceedings. Questions emerged as to why Erika's sister Azura, who was at home when everything happened, did not do anything to prevent the crime. From the images shown on television, it was evident that the house was not large enough for the noises of a very violent event, in which shouts and falling objects were surely generated, to have not been heard.

Why did Erika not do anything to defend her siblings either? She saw the crimes and, according to tests, the violence committed against her seemed to have been performed after the children were killed. As mentioned before, there are also people who suggest that Santoy had a sexual relationship with Teresa Coss, Erika's mother, and that the crime was Erika's revenge on her mother, where she and the so-called "killer of Cumbres" had a criminal and suicide pact that was not successfully carried out. In addition, other questions emerged as to why an eyewitness was left alive. Could it perhaps have been an attempt to retain contact with reality or to repent, or was it simply the clumsy behavior of a first-time killer?

Any attempt to understand the behavior of Santoy has to start with an analysis of his family upbringing. As mentioned before, there is a direct association between the development of psychiatric problems, physical mistreatment, and the sexual and emotional abuse of children. It is highly probable that the origins of this personality originated in his childhood. Television images portrayed his father as dominant, cold, and manipulative and his mother as submissive and a little expressive.

Borderline personalities are often in contact with other people with personality disorders. Therefore, the attitudes of the Peña Coss family with regard to the case are very revealing. The members of the family have demonstrated a certain inexplicable tranquility—being indifferent and detached—which to most would be unthinkable after the terrible violence experienced and the resulting coverage of which they were a part. In addition, on more than one occasion they have contradicted themselves in interviews.

An in-depth analysis of the fundamental factor that triggered these terrible actions is still pending. As we know, jealousy can be a manifestation of love, and it is possible that it can be a positive emotion if the accepted rules of the couple are respected. However, pathological jealousy is often accompanied by intense feelings of insecurity, self-pity, hostility, and depression, and can be destructive for relationships. It is also a factor that often leads to violence (da Costa et al., 2014).

Antisocial Personality

It is very common to hear the term *antisocial personality* or *sociopathy* when reference is made to violence and associated disorders. People who have antisocial personality often have chronic problems and their symptoms vary: they could be people who ask for loans constantly, "black sheep," pathological liars, white-collar criminals, people who hit their partners, or, at its most extreme, serial killers (Patrick, 2005; Semple, 2005).

When talking about this disorder, we are talking not about people who suffer from angry outbursts or who commit crimes of passion, but rather about those people who show, from a psychiatric point of view, a continuous pattern of rule breaking and violation of other people's rights, which normally starts before the age of 15 years. According to the *Diagnostic and Statistical Manual of Mental Disorders* (American Psychiatric Association, 1994, 2013), antisocial personality is more frequently seen in men than in women. The ratio of men to women who have been arrested for murder is 5:1, with the most common age group being 14–24 years old. The *DSM* points out that distinctive characteristics of those who suffer from this disorder include a lack of planning, changes of mood, the need to get immediate rewards, and the desire for confirmation of their superiority in all contexts. The final feature in this list means that they show exploitative behavior through the abuse of, envy towards, or devaluation of other people. Other features that are common include impulsiveness, a low frustration tolerance, an inability to tolerate routine or to have responsibilities, irritability, aggressiveness, and distrust.

The origin of the aggressive behavior of these individuals has been explained through a variety of paradigms that emphasize the role of frustration, a lack of control, and the absence of patterns of alternative behaviors, and include causal external attribution, modeling in adolescence, and situational stress, among others. The treatment of this disorder is equally complex, as pointed out by María González and Alejandra Ferrándiz, therapists in the Department of Applied Psychology at the UNED in Madrid, Spain (González & Ferrándiz, 2012). Due to the complexity of this personality disorder, multi-component treatments have been proposed for rehabilitation, which take into account the context, thoughts (distortions, justifications), feelings (frustration, anxiety, guilt, jealousy, exploitation), and behaviors (impulsiveness, isolation, dependency, inappropriate communication, self-destruction, unilateral decisions) that exist in aggressive personalities, especially in individuals who maltreat others. From a psychological perspective, these personalities feel a particular sense of freedom. For them, the fact of being free is equivalent to being able to do what they want in a specific moment without impediments. We know that limitations or actions can be internal or external. If these individuals minimize their internal limitations (controls), external limitations are then all that remain.

According to their reasoning, if external impediments are not corroborated by their own logic or feelings, then there is no reason to follow them. The rules of behavior and social interaction are considered artificial and generated by other people: a game where rules and obstacles are known, but are not followed. Nowadays, prisons around the world are full of these individuals.

An Example: The Case of Juan Luis Rojas López

Juan was born in Mexico City in November 1987. He is an only child and comes from a family where both he and his mother were mistreated by his father; this mistreatment was characterized both by verbal insults and by physical violence. Today, Juan is serving a sentence for murder in a high-security prison, as he cannot control his temperament and has caused several fights with other prison inmates.

Since he was a little boy, he has had problems of impulsiveness and aggressiveness, which have increased. Juan reports that he often "explodes" with verbal and physical aggression, particularly when he is in certain situations, such as if he feels he is being evaluated, if an "authority" figure gives him an order (as this makes him remember his father's abuse), or if he thinks that he is losing his position in a group or that his rights are not being respected. In his most recent argument, which was caused by a discussion about money, he hit his rival over the head with a bottle and then hit him with a chair.

His career as a criminal started at the age of 14 when, to get money to buy clothes, he started stealing car parts. Frequently, he escaped from his house and did not attend school. He often challenged his parents', teachers', and prefects' authority. He was expelled from school because he hit one of his teachers. He left high school and dedicated himself to working as a mechanic in an automobile repair shop, but, as he did not earn enough money, he began to sell drugs outside the school.

At the age of 16, he decided to live with a former classmate and he had three children with her. He had frequent problems with his partner, especially sexually, as he was very insistent and became angry if he did not feel satisfied. He had other relationships at the same time, but he says that he ended these relationships because he felt guilty and worried about being abandoned by his partner.

After he was arrested, Juan declared himself guilty. Nowadays, he says he is regretful. It is evident that he suffers from antisocial personality disorder, as he has shown a continuous pattern of rule breaking and violation of other people's rights, which started before he was 15 years old and has continued into adulthood. He finds it difficult to understand social rules and shows impulsiveness, aggressiveness, and irresponsibility. However, Juan cannot be classified as a psychopath (see Chapter 4), because he does not show emotional alterations, is able to form and keep affective relationships, and undoubtedly experiences feelings of empathy and guilt.

Primary Violence

In an individual displaying violent behavior, the violence is classed as primary if possible causes of secondary violence have been excluded. In other words, it is considered as primary violence when the violence is not linked to external or circumstantial factors.

From a biological point of view, aggressive behavior increases in complexity as it ascends in phylogenetic scale (Vonk & Shackelford, 2012). A variety of classifications of animal and human aggression have been proposed (e.g. Babcock et al., 2014; Kockler et al., 2006; Mathias et al., 2007; Weinshenker & Siegel, 2002). A frequent distinction is made between predatory, impulsive, and premeditated aggression. Predatory aggression is similar to an attack "in cold blood"; a predator is an animal that kills other species to eat them. This behavior is at least similar to premeditated aggression (e.g. in organized crimes), whereas impulsive aggression is more similar to an uncontrolled fit of anger. This final behavior is also known as "reactive" or "affective" aggression, in which a frustrating or threatening event triggers the aggressive act and often involves anger. A relevant distinction is that this form of aggression does not involve consideration of the potential target (e.g. by taking the victim's possessions away or by increasing the perpetrator's status within a particular group); by contrast, it is triggered only in a situation of ire.

By contrast, premeditated aggression, which is also known as "instrumental" or "proactive" aggression, involves a specific purpose and target. Generally, the perpetrator does not want the victim to experience pain, but does want the victim's possessions, social status, or respect within a particular group. A variety of studies have shown that it is premeditated or instrumental aggression, not impulsive or reactive aggression, that predicts if an individual is going to be a serial offender (Brendgen et al., 2001; Cornell et al., 1996; Murrie et al., 2004).

Moreover, there are considerable data that suggest that two independent populations of aggressive individuals exist (Anderson & Huesmann, 2003):

1. *Individuals who show only reactive aggression.* These individuals are characterized by being indifferent to conventions and social rules and not modulating their behavior according to the status of the individuals with whom they interact. Individuals with lesions in orbitofrontal areas with disorders of impulsive aggression and children with bipolar disorders can show high levels of reactive aggression.
2. *Individuals who show high levels of reactive aggression and premeditated or instrumental aggression.* These are individuals who are particularly indifferent to moral transgressions and who show very little empathy towards their victims and feel no guilt. Psychopaths often show high levels of instrumental and reactive aggression.

In summary, there are two groups that can be distinguished according to their level of aggression: people who show only impulsive aggression and people who show both impulsive and instrumental aggression. It is very important to distinguish between them because these types of behaviors are regulated by different neurocognitive systems.

Impulsive Violence

Impulsive violence is an intermittent explosive disorder in individuals who are not normally aggressive (Meyer-Lindenberg et al., 2006). It is defined as uncontrolled aggression that is charged with great emotion. Individuals who show impulsive aggression or episodic fits of violence are a serious danger to themselves, their families, and society. We are talking about people who respond to a variety of psychosocial stressors, and the intensity of their fits can range from verbal to physical aggression and homicide too. Investigations suggest that impulsive aggression is associated with biological substrates that alter physiological activation. It has been proved that these sudden surges of activation induce an agitated state of impulsive aggressiveness that the individuals are absolutely unable to control. Pharmacological treatments such as phenytoin seem to lead to a decrease in the degree of impulsiveness and, consequently, in violent acts. Individuals with lesions in orbitofrontal areas and individuals with bipolar disorders can show high levels of reactive aggression (Berlin, Rolls, & Kischka, 2004; Swann et al., 2001, 2004).

Richard Davidson's team analyzed the cerebral images of a wide group of studies conducted with violent individuals or those who are predisposed to violence (Davidson, Putnam, & Larson, 2000). These studies were focused on people who had been diagnosed with aggressive alterations in their personality, on people who had suffered cerebral lesions in their childhood, and on declared murderers. The investigators discovered among most of the 500 subjects a series of common neurological characteristics related to a cerebral inability to regulate emotions in an appropriate manner. This association between violence and brain dysfunction opens a new pathway for the study and, possibly, treatment of violence and aggressiveness. One of the main conclusions to which this study of the neurobiology of emotions came was that there is an interrelation between several regions of the brain, specifically the orbitofrontal cortex, the anterior cingulate cortex, and the amygdala. The orbitofrontal cortex carries out a crucial function in the regulation of impulsive manifestations, while the anterior cingulate cortex recruits other regions of the brain in the response with regard to conflict (Figure 3.1).

Alterations in the prefrontal cortex, specifically in the orbitofrontal area, can modify an individual's ability to inhibit aggressive impulses and modulate emotional reactions. This region inhibits impulses that are produced in areas of the limbic system, specifically in the hypothalamus and the amygdala, where fear and aggression seemingly originate. When there is a disconnection between these primitive systems and orbitofrontal areas, the person could present serious difficulties in moderating his or her emotional reactions. The most classic example in the literature is the case of Phineas Gage (Harlow, 1869). Orbitofrontal regions are involved in decision making and in the development of moral behavior. Alterations

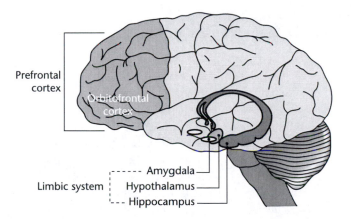

FIGURE 3.1   Brain regions that are related to the control of negative emotions are found in the prefrontal cortex

in these areas can explain the lack of empathy and repentance that are often characteristic of psychopaths, both criminals and non-criminals, who are able to plan and commit acts that manipulate and harm other people without showing any kind of remorse.

Premeditated Violence

By contrast to reactive or impulsive aggression, premeditated aggression is considered to be under the individual's control and is generally instrumental; in other words, a secondary benefit is obtained from the aggression. Premeditated aggression is characterized by planned and controlled acts and a lack of emotional content. This kind of violence implies a controlled aggressiveness that shows an instrumental nature; in other words, the violent act is planned and the execution of the act is methodical (Barratt & Felthous, 2003; Stanford et al., 2003).

Premeditated aggression is focused on a particular target and the aim is usually to get money from another person or to increase the perpetrator's status within a particular group. In fact, the majority of antisocial behaviors (theft, fraud, kidnapping) are instrumental and focused on a specific target. When a person reacts with instrumental aggression, it is probable that he or she uses the same neurocognitive systems that are required to perform planned motor behaviors.

The majority of individuals in a society are motivated by money and other benefits, but only a small proportion of people would be able to attack another person to obtain what they desire. Moral socialization leads healthy individuals away from antisocial behaviors. To explain why instrumental aggression is observed in psychopaths, it is important to understand the reasons why socialization is not achieved in these individuals.

Premeditated violence is basically observed in three different groups: serial killers, psychopaths, and terrorists.

Gender and Genes in Aggression

It is well accepted that a person's sex contributes significantly to aggression, with men generally more aggressive than women, particularly in a physical manner (Archer & Webb, 2006; Bettencourt & Miller, 1996; Campbell & Muncer, 2008). Gender is male and female identity shaped through what society sets as typical for each sex. Thus, gender is related to biological sex, but it involves the biopsychosociocultural distinctions between males and females: masculinity and femininity, respectively. In other words, gender refers to the stereotyped characteristics in a given situation of masculinity and femininity. Hence, people behave according to their internalized gender. Masculinity is often characterized by strength, control, independence, selfishness, and dominance, while femininity could be said to be characterized by emotions, nursing, tenderness, passivity, and obedience (Prakash et al., 2010; Rocha-Sánchez, 2005). However, traditional stereotypes are changing for men and women, and it is accepted that masculinity and femininity can coexist in the same individual, regardless of biological sex (Spence & Helmreich, 1978).

It has been suggested that people with a tightly defined masculine or executive identity are considered instrumental; people with a tightly defined feminine or expressive identity are considered expressive; people with a mixed identity (masculine and feminine) are considered androgynous; and people with a non-defined identity are considered undifferentiated (Rocha Sánchez, 2009). Previous research has shown the effects of gender on aggression. Most research claims that masculine or instrumental people, as well as androgynous people, are more aggressive (Kopper & Epperson, 1991), while people with a feminine or expressive identity show a negative correlation with aggressive traits. However, some researchers have suggested that feminine or expressive and undifferentiated people could have more aggressive, cognitive, and affective traits, such as hostility and anger (Reidy, Sloan, & Zeichner, 2009).

Another factor that explains individual differences in aggression is genes. Twin and adoption studies are consistent regarding the genetic contribution to aggression. It has been suggested that genetic factors explain about 50% of the variance, including aggressive, violent, antisocial, and criminal behaviors (Baker et al., 2008; Ferguson, 2010). However, there are factors that can affect this contribution, such as the severity of the behavior, age, biological sex, and the stability of the behavior over time. A larger genetic effect has been found in the case of more severe behaviors, in males, and at more advanced ages, and some studies have revealed that the genetic effect remains constant over time. Hence, aggression is partly heritable, but it is best explained by the gene–environment interaction (Raine, 2002).

There are no specific genes that code for aggression, but allelic variations could lead to differences in a person's susceptibility to aggression. A particular polymorphism has been well identified in research on genetic predisposition to aggression: the MAOA-uVNTR polymorphism (McDermott et al., 2009). It is a functional variable-number tandem repeat (VNTR) polymorphism in the upstream region of the gene that codifies for the enzyme monoamine oxidase A (MAOA). It consists in a sequence of 30 base-pair repeats with high-activity (MAOAH: 3.5 and 4 repeats) and low-activity (MAOAL: 2, 3 and 5 repeats) variants. As the enzyme is located in the outer mitochondrial membrane in the presynaptic terminal neuron and in astrocytes, the gene, which is mapped to adjacent sites on chromosome Xp11.23, participates in regulating the serotonin concentration in the brain, especially before birth because its enzyme is present at adult levels at this stage. The high-activity variants are associated with a lower concentration of serotonin and the low-activity variants with a higher concentration of serotonin (Buckholtz & Meyer-Lindenberg, 2008).

The first evidence that associated variations in the MAOA gene with aggression was a study of a mutation in a Dutch family. It was found that this mutation was leading to an enzymatic deficiency that caused retardation and impulsive aggression in men, as it was in an X-linked gene (Brunner et al., 1993). Afterwards, in a knock-out mouse model, it was confirmed that the enzymatic deficiency caused by the suppression of the MAOA gene caused increases in central serotonin and aggressive behavior in adult males (Cases et al., 1995). As a result, several studies have focused on the MAOA-uVNTR–environment interaction in relation to aggression. The findings remain unclear regarding whether MAOAH or MAOAL should be considered the variant that increases susceptibility to aggression. Although many studies claim that it is the MAOAL variant (Widom & Brzustowicz, 2006), a few, including a meta-analysis, claim that it is the MAOAH variant (McGrath et al., 2012). Therefore, more evidence is required to clarify this issue.

Castillo-López et al. (2015) selected 292 healthy undergraduates, who were assessed with an aggression questionnaire and an inventory for assessing gender characteristics. The genotyping technique was used to obtain the students' MAOA genotype. Main and interaction effects split by sex were analyzed by a two-way multivariate analysis of variance. It was found that androgynous traits had an effect on verbal aggression, anger, hostility, and total aggression in males and females, while instrumental traits had an effect on physical aggression in males. The MAOAH genotype had an effect on hostility in males and the MAOAL genotype had an effect on verbal aggression in females. Finally, a gender-related MAOA-uVNTR interaction was observed in relation to anger and total aggression in males. It was concluded that males are more likely to show anger and aggression when the predisposing genetic and environmental factors interact. Androgynous identity contributes to general aggression in both sexes, instrumental identity contributes to physical aggression in males, and undifferentiated identity leads to lower levels of aggression. These findings shed light on factors that could be initial indicators of future violence.

Other Expressions of Violence

Terrorism

Due to the wave of terrorist attacks that have been happening around the world, psychologists such as Aaron Beck, Director of the Center of Cognitive Therapy of New York, have tried to analyze why and how terrorists are mentally prepared both for their own death and for the death of innocent men, women, and children (Beck, 2002). What is the psychological state of terrorists? Their ideology dominates a significant proportion of what they do and think. They are able to assume a dual identity. They externally behave and act as the environment that is around them dictates; for example, one of the terrorists involved in the attack on the World Trade Center in New York on September 11, 2001, went to pubs and striptease clubs, which is against the Muslim faith. However, their central identity remains the same and they stay dedicated to acts of destruction that are programmed by their ideology.

Nevertheless, in addition to this dual identity, it is very significant to understand how these individuals perceive their victim(s). For terrorist groups, roles are inverted and, in their minds, they are the victims and the enemy is the executioner. The radicals of these groups see the target of their attack as a potent hostile power that threatens their existence. This way of thinking gives them energy and helps them to crystallize a mental representation that feeds the terrorist violence. For example, for the group Al-Qaeda, the West is a projection of the enemy: corrupt, addicted, and dangerous. As this image is solidified, their own collective image is exalted as "sacred," "good," and "right."

Religious and moral symbols permeate terrorist' thoughts. The image could take a dramatic shape: the forces of evil against the forces of good—for example, Satan against Allah or something similar. In their minds, the most viable solution is violence against their oppressors and those who are corrupt. Radicals, who are obsessed with these polarized images, turn to recruitment and to assigning the task of destroying other people. What they attack is the image of the enemy, which is projected onto innocent victims.

The thoughts of a terrorist include distortions and cognitive failures, such as those that are observed in people who perform violent acts; this is true both individually and as a group. Their view of the world has the following characteristics:

- *overgeneralization:* they presuppose that the sins of the enemy can be attributed to whole populations;
- *dichotomous thinking:* they believe that people are totally good or bad;
- *tunnel vision:* as soon as they are involved, their sacred and/or patriotic mission is the only target that they can visualize, and this includes the destruction of the enemy;
- *programming:* they behave as if they are programmed to destroy, without paying attention to the meaning of the lives that they destroy, including their own;
- *sense of heroism:* they gratify themselves with the "heroic" role that fate has granted them.

All or many of these characteristics have been or are present in combatants of a number of armies throughout history.

Abuse of Authority, Sadism, and Torture

Through the recent revelations about the incidents of abuse, sadism, and torture that North American soldiers carried out against inmates of Abu Ghraib prison in Iraq, questions have emerged about whether these behaviors are the result of personalities with psychiatric alterations of a sadomasochistic type or if they were terrifying actions carried out by ordinary and "mentally healthy" people.

Unfortunately, a number of psychological studies that were conducted in the School of Psychology at Stanford University have revealed, first, that this kind of behavior is common during military conflicts and, second, that the potential to abuse and maltreat other people resides inside all of us (Zimbardo, 2007).

The human being is born with willingness and basic feelings towards his or her fellow creatures, which can be modified, moderated, and expanded to produce pro-social behaviors; however, we are also born with a potential to manifest destructive, antisocial, and dehumanizing behaviors. Dehumanization and depersonalization, which are mechanisms of psychological defense, promote wars. To kill another human being, it is necessary to abolish all feeling of empathy and represent him or her as a wild and barbarous person whose aim is to cause us harm.

The bad news is that we are all able to manifest such behaviors. In a classic study developed by Philip Zimbardo (2007) and his colleagues at Stanford University, it was proved that the situation can have a powerful influence, as can the social definition of roles in that context. To carry out the investigation, 21 university students, who were found to be emotionally stable, physically healthy, mature, and observers of the law, were recruited to participate in a study about life in prison. Over a period of two weeks, 11 of them were designated randomly to act as prison guards and the other 10 were designated as prisoners. The latter group were captured by surprise, handcuffed, and had their fingerprints taken. They received uniforms with identification numbers and striped caps, and were imprisoned in cells of two by three meters without windows and in the basement of a building of the university. By contrast, official uniforms, reflective sunglasses (to avoid eye contact with the prison inmates), nightsticks, whistles, handcuffs, and keys were distributed to the prison guards.

However, the experiment worked "too well": overnight, the prison guards became authoritarian and abusive at a variety of levels. Some began acting in an arbitrary, hostile, and cruel manner, and used their new power to degrade and humiliate the prisoners, who, at the same time, were turning into passive people who gradually reacted and spoke less. The prisoners began to develop depression and anxiety, and psychosomatic eruptions began to appear on their bodies.

The volunteers, who did not show different personalities in the beginning, acquired traits related to their condition of being either prisoners or prison guards. In the same way as in the case of the prisoners in Iraq, the prison guards started to undress the prisoners and mock them, among other things, to humiliate and confuse them. According to Zimbardo, these expressions of abuse and sadism can be linked to the dynamic of the group and to the circumstances, not to individual personality. In the opinion of the experts, to change the existing undesirable behavior of subjects, we must first determine the institutional supports that sustain that behavior and then design and implement programs to alter these environments.

Pathological Jealousy

Jealousy is an emotion that emerges, for example, when somebody wants to possess their beloved person exclusively. The fear of the real or imaginary loss is manifested as a threat. We normally associate this feeling with relationships with partners, but it can also exist among siblings, coworkers, classmates, and friends (Kast, 1991).

Jealousy and envy have the same motive: the need to possess. However, there is a key distinction between them. A jealous person manifests a fear of losing his or her possession; in other words, he or she considers that it belongs to him or her and does not want anybody to take it away. By contrast, an envious person wants to have what he or she does not own. The pathology of jealousy has its origin in the personality itself of the jealous person. Jealousy is a feeling that is seen in both men and women, and its underlying emotional issues often manifest in a serious problem of low self-esteem. In fact, men and women experience jealousy at the same frequency and intensity, but it often manifests in different ways: men show aggression whereas women become depressed. Women often react hysterically or feel discouraged, whereas men often display paranoid and obsessive symptoms that are more difficult to control.

A variety of therapies have been tried for subjects with pathological jealousy (e.g. Ellis, 1996). As a jealous man believes that he has exclusive rights over his partner, many of his violent acts are the result of the incorrect perception that his partner could abandon him; consequently, to correct his behavior, that incorrect perception must be modified. This therapy consists in helping him to recover his dignity and to elevate his self-esteem and confidence in himself and his partner. Part of this therapy involves helping him to understand that it is impossible to have confidence in another person if that person does not have confidence in him- or herself. The first step involves the jealous person recognizing his or her pathology. From there, the treatment to overcome the problem is performed separately. The key is that the jealous person learns to control his or her thoughts, and also that his or her partner knows the techniques required to avoid further conflict. On many occasions, the victim of the pathological jealousy decides to lie to avoid his or her partner's anger or aggression; however, the most probable outcome from this is in fact the opposite: that the partner's suspicions will increase.

References

American Psychiatric Association—Task Force on DSM-IV (1994). *Diagnostic and Statistical Manual of Mental Disorders: DSM-IV*. Washington, DC: American Psychiatric Association.

American Psychiatric Association—Work Group on Borderline Personality Disorder (2001). *Practice Guideline for the Treatment of Patients with Borderline Personality Disorder*. Washington, DC: American Psychiatric Association.

American Psychiatric Association (2013). *DSM 5*. Washington, DC: American Psychiatric Association.

Anderson, C.A., & Huesmann, L.R. (2003). Human aggression: A social-cognitive view. In: Hogg, M.A., & Cooper, J. (eds), *The SAGE Handbook of Social Psychology*. Thousand Oaks, CA: SAGE Publications. pp. 296–323.

Anderson, P.D., & Bokor, G. (2012). Forensic aspects of drug-induced violence. *Journal of Pharmacy Practice*, 25(1), 41–49.

Archer, J., & Webb, I.A. (2006). The relation between scores on the Buss–Perry Aggression Questionnaire and aggressive acts, impulsiveness, competitiveness, dominance, and sexual jealousy. *Aggressive Behavior*, 32(5), 464–473.

Ardila, A., Rosselli, M., & Strumwasser, S. (1991). Neuropsychological deficits in chronic cocaine abusers. *International Journal of Neuroscience*, 57(1–2), 73–79.

Babcock, J.C., Tharp, A.L., Sharp, C., Heppner, W., & Stanford, M.S. (2014). Similarities and differences in impulsive/premeditated and reactive/proactive bimodal classifications of aggression. *Aggression and Violent Behavior*, 19(3), 251–262.

Baker, L.A., Raine, A., Liu, J., & Jacobson, K.C. (2008). Differential genetic and environmental influences on reactive and proactive aggression in children. *Journal of Abnormal Child Psychology*, 36(8), 1265–1278.

Barratt, E.S., & Felthous, A.R. (2003). Impulsive versus premeditated aggression: Implications for *mens rea* decisions. *Behavioral Sciences & the Law*, 21(5), 619–630.

Beck, A.T. (2002). Prisoners of hate. *Behavior Research and Therapy*, 40(3), 209–216.

Berlin, H.A., Rolls, E.T., & Kischka, U. (2004). Impulsivity, time perception, emotion and reinforcement sensitivity in patients with orbitofrontal cortex lesions. *Brain*, 127(5), 1108–1126.

Bettencourt, B., & Miller, N. (1996). Gender differences in aggression as a function of provocation: A meta-analysis. *Psychological Bulletin*, 119(3), 422–447.

Brendgen, M., Vitaro, F., Tremblay, R.E., & Lavoie, F. (2001). Reactive and proactive aggression: Predictions to physical violence in different contexts and moderating effects of parental monitoring and caregiving behavior. *Journal of Abnormal Child Psychology*, 29(4), 293–304.

Brunner, H.G., Nelen, M., Breakefield, X.O., Ropers, H.H., & Van Oost, B.A. (1993). Abnormal behavior associated with a point mutation in the structural gene for monoamine oxidase A. *Science*, 262(5133), 578–580.

Buckholtz, J.W., & Meyer-Lindenberg, A. (2008). MAOA and the neurogenetic architecture of human aggression. *Trends in Neurosciences*, 31(3), 120–129.

Campbell, A., & Muncer, S. (2008). Intent to harm or injure? Gender and the expression of anger. *Aggressive Behavior*, 34(3), 282–293.

Cases, O., Seif, I., Grimsby, J., Gaspar, P., Chen, K., Pournin, S., ... & De Maeyer, E. (1995). Aggressive behavior and altered amounts of brain serotonin and norepinephrine in mice lacking MAOA. *Science*, 268(5218), 1763–1766.

Castillo-López, G., Ostrosky, F., Camarena-Medellín, B., & Vélez-García, A.E. (2015). Moderating effect of gender and MAOA genotype on aggression and violence. *Revista Médica del Hospital General de México*, 78(1), 4–12.

Cechova-Vayleux, E., Leveillee, S., Lhuillier, J.P., Garre, J.B., Senon, J.L., & Richard-Devantoy, S. (2013). Singularités cliniques et criminologiques de l'uxoricide: Eléments de compréhension du meurtre conjugal [Female intimate partner homicide: Clinical and criminological issues]. *L'Encephale*, 39(6), 416–425.

Chilcoat, H.D., & Breslau, N. (1998). Investigations of causal pathways between PTSD and drug use disorders. *Addictive Behaviors*, 23(6), 827–840.

Coccaro, E.F., Kavoussi, R.J., Trestman, R.L., Gabriel, S.M., Cooper, T.B., & Siever, L.J. (1997). Serotonin function in human subjects: Intercorrelations among central 5-HT indices and aggressiveness. *Psychiatry Research*, 73(1), 1–14.

Cornell, D.G., Warren, J., Hawk, G., Stafford, E., Oram, G., & Pine, D. (1996). Psychopathy in instrumental and reactive violent offenders. *Journal of Consulting and Clinical Psychology*, 64(4), 783–790.

da Costa, A.L., Sophia, E.C., Sanches, C., Tavares, H., & Zilberman, M.L. (2014). Pathological jealousy: Romantic relationship characteristics, emotional and personality aspects, and social adjustment. *Journal of Affective Disorders*, 15(174), 38–44.

Davidson, R.J., Putnam, K.M., & Larson, C.L. (2000). Dysfunction in the neural circuitry of emotion regulation: A possible prelude to violence. *Science*, 289(5479), 591–594.

Ellis, A. (1996). The treatment of morbid jealousy: A rational emotive behavior therapy approach. *Journal of Cognitive Psychotherapy*, 10(1), 23–33.

Fava, M., & Rosenbaum, J.F. (1999). Anger attacks in patients with depression. *Journal of Clinical Psychiatry*, 60(Suppl. 15), 21–24.

Ferguson, C.J. (2010). Genetic contributions to antisocial personality and behavior: A meta-analytic review from an evolutionary perspective. *The Journal of Social Psychology*, 150(2), 160–180.

Ferguson, C.J., & Beaver, K.M. (2009). Natural born killers: The genetic origins of extreme violence. *Aggression and Violent Behavior*, 14(5), 286–294.

Fromm, E. (1973). *The Anatomy of Human Destructiveness*. New York, NY: Holt, Rinehart & Winston.

González, M., & Ferrándiz, A. (2012). Prevención de la escalada de violencia en un paciente con personalidad antisocial [Prevention of the escalation of violence in a case of antisocial personality]. *Acción Psicológica*, 2(1), 87–98.

Harlow, J.M. (1869). *Recovery from the Passage of an Iron Bar Through the Head*. Boston, MA: David Clapp & Son.

Hawkins, A.A., Furr, R.M., Arnold, E.M., Law, M.K., Mneimne, M., & Fleeson, W. (2014). The structure of borderline personality disorder symptoms: A multi-method, multi-sample examination. *Personality Disorders: Theory, Research, and Treatment*, 5(4), 380.

Kast, R. (1991). Pathological jealousy defined. *The British Journal of Psychiatry*, 159(4), 590.

Kirschbaum, K.M., Grigoleit, L., Hess, C., Madea, B., & Musshoff, F. (2013). Illegal drugs and delinquency. *Forensic Science International*, 226(1), 230–234.

Kockler, T.R., Stanford, M.S., Nelson, C.E., Meloy, J.R., & Sanford, K. (2006). Characterizing aggressive behavior in a forensic population. *American Journal of Orthopsychiatry*, 76(1), 80–85.

Komarekova, I., & Janik, M. (2012). Effects of alcohol on the brain biomembranes: A review. *Soudni Lekarstvi*, 57(4), 75–77.

Kopper, B.A., & Epperson, D.L. (1991). Sex and sex-role comparisons in the expression of anger. *Psychology of Women Quarterly*, 15(1), 7–14.

Larsen, R.J., & Buss, D.M. (2008). *Personality Psychology*. Jastrebarsko, Croatia: Naklada Slap.

Leggio, L., Kenna, G.A., & Swift, R.M. (2008). New developments for the pharmacological treatment of alcohol withdrawal syndrome: A focus on non-benzodiazepine GABAergic medications. *Progress in Neuro-Psychopharmacology and Biological Psychiatry*, 32(5), 1106–1117.

Lin, H.L., Lin, T.Y., Soo, K.M., Chen, C.W., Kuo, L.C., Lin, Y.K., ... & Lin, C.L. (2014). The effect of alcohol intoxication on mortality of blunt head injury. *BioMed Research International*, 2014: 619231.

Mathias, C.W., Stanford, M.S., Marsh, D.M., Frick, P.J., Moeller, F.G., Swann, A.C., & Dougherty, D.M. (2007). Characterizing aggressive behavior with the Impulsive/ Premeditated Aggression Scale among adolescents with conduct disorder. *Psychiatry Research*, 151(3), 231–242.

McCann, U.D., Szabo, Z., Seckin, E., Rosenblatt, P., Mathews, W.B., Ravert, H.T., ... & Ricaurte, G.A. (2005). Quantitative PET studies of the serotonin transporter in MDMA users and controls using [11C] McN5652 and [11C] DASB. *Neuropsychopharmacology*, 30(9), 1741–1750.

McDermott, R., Tingley, D., Cowden, J., Frazzetto, G., & Johnson, D.D. (2009). Monoamine oxidase A gene (MAOA) predicts behavioral aggression following provocation. *Proceedings of the National Academy of Sciences*, 106(7), 2118–2123.

McGrath, L.M., Mustanski, B., Metzger, A., Pine, D.S., Kistner-Griffin, E., Cook, E., & Wakschlag, L.S. (2012). A latent modeling approach to genotype–phenotype relationships: Maternal problem behavior clusters, prenatal smoking, and MAOA genotype. *Archives of Women's Mental Health*, 15(4), 269–282.

Meyer-Lindenberg, A., Buckholtz, J.W., Kolachana, B., Hariri, A.R., Pezawas, L., Blasi, G., ... & Weinberger, D.R. (2006). Neural mechanisms of genetic risk for impulsivity and violence in humans. *FOCUS: The Journal of Lifelong Learning in Psychiatry*, 4(3), 360–368.

Murrie, D.C., Cornell, D.G., Kaplan, S., McConville, D., & Levy-Elkon, A. (2004). Psychopathy scores and violence among juvenile offenders: A multi-measure study. *Behavioral Sciences & the Law*, 22(1), 49–67.

Patrick, C. (2005). *Handbook of Psychopathy*. New York, NY: Guilford Press.

Prakash, J., Kotwal, A.S.M., Ryali, V.S.S.R., Srivastava, K., Bhat, P.S., & Shashikumar, R. (2010). Does androgyny have psychoprotective attributes? A cross-sectional community-based study. *Industrial Psychiatry Journal*, 19(2), 119–124.

Raine, A. (2002). The biological basis of crime. In: Wilson, J.Q., & Petersilia, J. (eds), *Crime: Public Policies for Crime Control*. Oakland, CA: ICS Press. pp. 43–74.

Rapoport, A. (1994). *The Origins of Violence: Approaches to the Study of Conflict*. New Brunswick, NJ: Transaction Publishers.

Reidy, D.E., Sloan, C.A., & Zeichner, A. (2009). Gender role conformity and aggression: Influence of perpetrator and victim conformity on direct physical aggression in women. *Personality and Individual Differences*, 46(2), 231–235.

Rocha-Sánchez, T.E. (2005). Cultura de género: La brecha ideológica entre hombres y mujeres [Gender culture: The ideological gap between men and women]. *Anales de Psicología*, 21(1), 42–49.

Rocha-Sánchez, T.E. (2009). Desarrollo de la identidad de género desde una perspectiva psico-socio-cultural: Un recorrido conceptual [Development of gender identity from a psycho-socio-cultural perspective: A conceptual approach]. *Interamerican Journal of Psychology*, 43(2), 250–259.

Rosselli, M., & Ardila, A. (1996). Cognitive effects of cocaine and polydrug abuse. *Journal of Clinical and Experimental Neuropsychology*, 18(1), 122–135.

Semple, D. (2005). *The Oxford Handbook of Psychiatry*. New York, NY: Oxford University Press.

Spence, J.T., & Helmreich, R.L. (1978). *Masculinity & Femininity: Their Psychological Dimensions, Correlates, and Antecedents*. Austin, TX: University of Texas Press.

Stanford, M.S., Houston, R.J., Villemarette-Pittman, N.R., & Greve, K.W. (2003). Premeditated aggression: Clinical assessment and cognitive psychophysiology. *Personality and Individual Differences*, 34(5), 773–781.

Staub, E. (1989). *The Roots of Evil: The Origins of Genocide and Other Group Violence*. Cambridge, UK: Cambridge University Press.

Staub, E. (1999). The origins and prevention of genocide, mass killing, and other collective violence. *Peace and Conflict: Journal of Peace Psychology*, 5(4), 303–336.

Swann, A.C., Anderson, J.C., Dougherty, D.M., & Moeller, F.G. (2001). Measurement of inter-episode impulsivity in bipolar disorder. *Psychiatry Research*, 101(2), 195–197.

Swann, A.C., Dougherty, D.M., Pazzaglia, P.J., Pham, M., & Moeller, F.G. (2004). Impulsivity: A link between bipolar disorder and substance abuse. *Bipolar Disorders*, 6(3), 204–212.

Vonk, J., & Shackelford, T.K. (eds). (2012). *The Oxford Handbook of Comparative Evolutionary Psychology*. New York, NY: Oxford University Press.

Weinshenker, N.J., & Siegel, A. (2002). Bimodal classification of aggression: Affective defense and predatory attack. *Aggression and Violent Behavior*, 7(3), 237–250.

Widom, C.S., & Brzustowicz, L.M. (2006). MAOA and the "cycle of violence": Childhood abuse and neglect, MAOA genotype, and risk for violent and antisocial behavior. *Biological Psychiatry*, 60(7), 684–689.

Wrangham, R.W., & Peterson, D. (1996). *Demonic Males: Apes and the Origins of Human Violence*. Boston, MA: Houghton Mifflin Harcourt.

Zimbardo, P. (2007). *The Lucifer Effect: Understanding How Good People Turn Evil*. New York, NY: Random House.

4
PSYCHOPATHY

Introduction

Psychopathic behaviors have been an object of fascination throughout history. We can all think of a psychopath, whether real or fictional. Some people think of movie characters such as Hannibal Lecter, played by Anthony Hopkins in *The Silence of the Lambs*; others think of genocidal figures from history such as Adolf Hitler or of more contemporary, closer-to-home criminals such as Timothy McVeigh, whose crimes induce horror and defiance, and, at the same time, cause great curiosity.

Even though psychopaths are mentally disturbed people, it cannot be said that they have lost their sense of reality. In other words, psychopaths do not present serious alterations in thought and perception, such as hallucinations or distorted thoughts, which are characteristic of schizophrenics (Patrick, 2005). A first and important point is that psychopathy is not a cognitive disorder, but a personality disorder (Lilienfeld, 2011).

Personality Disorders

Personality is our way of being, our particular form of behavior. Psychopathy is a way of acting in the world. Personality disorders are patterns of behavior and relationships with the environment that are relatively stable, inflexible, and, most importantly, socially inappropriate, and that involve a great diversity of situations (Millon & Davis, 1996). Psychopaths can be apparently normal people. Their coldness, selfishness, and propensity for lying distinguish their social relationships at all levels. In spite of these characteristics, they can act with great superficial charm, which, in conjunction with their moral flexibility and lack of remorse, frequently allows them to be very socially successful (Hare & Neumann, 2009).

The personality disorder from which psychopaths suffer is simultaneously manifested in three ways: in their relationships with others, in their affectivity, and in their behavior. In the first of these, psychopaths tend to manipulate and deceive others. In relation to their affectivity, they lack empathy—they are unable to put themselves into another's place. As regards their behavior, they can be antisocial, although also can appear to be kind and seductive.

Psychopaths are responsible for a large proportion of the conflicts that exist in our surroundings, as they often alter the lives of people around them in a negative way. A classic, and unfortunately very frequent, example is husbands who are externally charming and successful at work, but at home are cold and selfish and do not interest themselves in their children's or partner's lives. Many of these men are dominant figures who keep their wives "in chains" by subjecting them to constant physical and psychological abuse (Bismuth, 2010).

Not All Psychopaths Are Criminals

The image that we have of a psychopath, which has largely been created by the media (that of a predator who searches, spies on, captures, tortures, and cold-bloodedly kills his or her victim without remorse), corresponds to the character of only some of these individuals, not all. Many psychopaths never commit violent crimes. As in all personality disorders, various levels of severity are shown: in some cases, it can be mild; in others, it can be extreme.

From a clinical perspective, being a psychopath does not mean being a criminal (Patrick, 2005). In fact, many of the individuals who suffer from this personality disorder never go to jail. Some of them are informal workers, unscrupulous businessmen, corrupt politicians, or professionals who act with a complete lack of ethics and who use their prestige and power to victimize their clients, patients, or society in general.

Psychopathic personalities can live ordinary lives (Thompson, Ramos, & Willett, 2014). They can work, get married, and be notable professionals, but the traits of their personality stop their job and marriage from lasting. Robert Hare, Professor of Forensic Psychology at the University of British Columbia, points out that, in Canada, between 25% and 30% of husbands who often mistreat their wives and at present are in a treatment program imposed by a court are psychopaths (Hare & Neumann, 2009).

Another characteristic of psychopaths is that they often have chaotic personal lives: they are almost always in trouble or near it. Moreover, psychopathic personalities satisfy their needs by following their own rules and using other people as objects.

Another relevant fact is that most psychopaths are male. According to the *Diagnostic and Statistical Manual of Mental Disorders* (American Psychiatric Association, 1994, 2013), men are three times more likely to present psychopathy than women and, in both sexes, it occurs more frequently in the age range between 25 and 44 years old.

The ambivalent characteristics of psychopathic personality have meant this phenomenon has been a worry since ancient times. There are records of people whose behavior has been regarded as strange but who could not be categorized as either "insane" or "sane." Philippe Pinel (1806), who is considered by many to be the founder of modern psychiatry, was the first person to use the clinical concept of psychopathy by coining the term *manie sans délire* ("mania without delirium") to diagnose those people who showed an uncontrolled rage and had normal intellectual function.

Later, James Prichard (1837), an English psychiatrist, introduced the concept of "moral insanity" with which he referred to a madness in moral judgment rather than a madness affecting intelligence. In 1941, American psychiatrist H. Cleckley (1941) wrote a book entitled *The Mask of Sanity* making reference to this kind of person. In history, there have been cases such as Jack the Ripper, the alias of the sadly notorious serial killer who was active in London in 1888 and who strangled and mutilated five prostitutes. According to the London Metropolitan Police report, Jack's murders were typically perpetrated in a public or semi-public place (Curtis, 2008). The victims' throats were cut from left to right (which suggested that he was right-handed), followed by abdominal mutilation, although in some cases these mutilations were extended to other parts of the body. Many people believe that the victims were previously strangled to silence them. Due to the nature of the wounds, it has been proposed that the killer had some knowledge of anatomy, so he could have been a doctor or a butcher. Researchers believe that he was well behaved in public and had an innate capacity to blend into a crowd, and have come to the conclusion that he was surely interrogated by the police, who disregarded him because his normal aspect did not reveal a sadistic person like the one for which they were looking. The famous Jack was never captured but, according to Scotland Yard's documents, one of the main suspects was a barber called Aaron Kosminski.

Psychopaths have been informally described as "humans without a soul." This lack of spiritual quality turns them into, in some ways, very efficient machines. Because of these characteristics, it is very common to find a close relationship between psychopathy and antisocial behavior (Hare, 1996; Hare & Neumann, 2009; Semple & Smyth, 2013). Although, as mentioned before, not all psychopaths fall into delinquency and criminality, it is a fact that, when it does happen, they are different from other criminals because their behavior has a very predatory character: they see other people as emotional, physical, and economic prey. Psychopaths predominate among the serial killers who plan murders "in cold blood." They have a great ability to camouflage themselves (to deceive and manipulate) and to stalk and locate a "hunting ground." They often ritualize their murders, with the final act being to take a trophy of the victim, symbolized in a garment or another object that they take as a memento. An example is the case of the Colombian Luis Alfredo Garavito, who killed more than 200 children (and maybe more than 400) in the 1990s (*Encyclopaedia Britannica*, n.d.). This pederast and serial killer used to take as trophies the photographs of the children's identity cards that are used in Colombia, and collected them inside a wooden box.

However, whether or not psychopaths become serial killers, it is true that there are many who are delinquents. *Rethinking Risk Assessment: The MacArthur Study of Mental Disorder and Violence* (Monahan et al., 2001), the broadest and most exhaustive research that has been conducted on this subject, reports that the incidence of psychopathy in the normal population ranges from 1% to 3%, while in the convict population the percentage of individuals suffering from psychopathy can reach up to 25%.

Likewise, investigations by Robert Hare's team at the University of British Columbia (Hare, 1999a; Hare & Neumann, 2009) show that, among psychopaths, the rate of recidivism is very high. In other words, within six years of release, more than 80% of psychopaths reoffend in a violent way, in contrast with only 20% of those who do not present this disorder. Cold and unscrupulous violence often increases in intensity in recidivism.

Emotionally Underactivated

From a biological point of view, psychopaths are considered to be physiologically underactivated; that is, they are people who experience less fear and anxiety than normal people. This was demonstrated by the psychologist Christopher Patrick (Patrick, 2005; Patrick & Bernat, 2009; Patrick & Berthot, 1995; Patrick & Zempolich, 1999; Patrick, Bradley, & Lang, 1993; Patrick, Cuthbert, & Lang, 1994), who with his collaborators conducted an experiment with normal and psychopathic subjects. In this research, the activation level of the subjects was obtained through the record of the galvanic skin response (GSR). This measures the activation of the sweat glands of the skin, which is associated with emotional state (as the palms sweat in critical situations). The higher the gland activation, the higher the GSR. The participants had to find out which of four levers turned on a green light bulb. However, if the person activated one of the wrong levers, he or she immediately received an electric shock as penalization. Patrick discovered that both groups made the same number of mistakes, but the sane group presented a very large GSR and learned to avoid the electric shocks faster, while the psychopaths did not show this response and they took more time to achieve this. Apparently, they were underactivated: the punishment did not provoke affective responses. It is this need for strong emotions that causes the psychopath to look for dangerous situations.

A Psychopath's Brain

Current neuroimaging techniques (especially positron emission tomography (PET) and functional magnetic resonance imaging (fMRI)) allow brain structures to be studied in detail, along with the changes associated with emotional processing produced in the brain (Decety et al., 2013). Using these techniques, it has been confirmed that there are killers who do actually commit their crimes in cold blood; that is, they experience little or no emotion when killing their victims. These kinds of individuals are the opposite of passionate killers, who can be named "warm blooded" and who kill their victims in a moment of uncontrolled emotion. The question here is whether the "predator assassin" possesses a more regulated and controlled brain functionality compared to the "impulsive assassin," who kills in a moment of passion without regulation or brain control.

Adrian Raine, Professor of Psychology at the University of Southern California, and his team used neuroimaging techniques to investigate if there are differences in brain activity between these two forms of aggression (Raine et al., 1998). They divided the studied killers into two groups: 15 predatory individuals and nine affective individuals. The first group was made up of controlled killers who planned their crimes, lacked affectivity, and attacked strangers. Those in the second group were affective killers who acted in a much less planned way, under very intense emotion, and, mainly, in their own homes. Raine and his team found that the affective killers' prefrontal cortex showed low activity rates. We must be reminded here that it is precisely in this part of the brain that the mechanism that controls aggressive impulses is located. By contrast, the investigations showed that the predatory killers exhibited relatively normal prefrontal function. Therefore, this corroborated the hypothesis that an intact prefrontal cortex allows predatory killers to keep their behavior under control, while adapting it in this way to their antisocial purposes. Raine and his team also concluded that, in comparison with normal people, both killer groups showed higher activity rates in the structures that integrate the "emotional brain" (the limbic system), including the amygdala, the hippocampus, and the hypothalamus. Apparently, due to the activity excess in these structures, killers from both groups could be more likely to behave aggressively. However, what distinguished predators from affective killers was that they had a prefrontal function that was normal enough to enable them to regulate their aggressive impulses and to be able to manipulate others to achieve their own targets. In addition, as affective killers lack prefrontal control over their impulses, they experienced aggressive, impulsive, and uncontrolled outbursts.

In this same study, it was also discovered that, in some cases, it was not brain structures, but interconnection fibers that were affected. In other words, there was inefficient communication between the prefrontal and emotional areas of the brain (Raine & Yang, 2006; Yang & Raine, 2009). This inefficient brain communication could also be associated with mistreatment experienced during the early stages of life. Some studies, such as the one by Joan McCord (2007), have pointed out that the great majority of violent delinquents come from homes where they have suffered from some kind of mistreatment. There is a hypothesis that states that if a baby is abruptly shaken in a repeated way (known as "shaken baby syndrome"; American Academy of Pediatrics, 2001), it is very likely that the white fibers that link the brain cortex to other structures are broken, leaving the rest of the brain free from prefrontal control. Other factors that could cause this same breaking of the fibers and affect the brain morphology of the baby are alcoholism of the mother and drug addiction during pregnancy (McCord, 2007).

Other studies have shown that some violent killers show high levels of testosterone (Mazur, 2006, 2008). This hormone is related to extroversion, sociability behaviors, and the search for extreme experiences and sensations, as well as escape from monotony. However, it has also been determined that testosterone itself is not responsible for acting with aggression, and it is known that testosterone decreases the threshold to trigger aggression. Moreover, it has been discovered that our level of impulsivity depends, partly, on serotonin levels in the brain (Dalley & Roiser, 2012). The concentration of this neurotransmitter can decrease because of the consumption of alcohol. At the same time, our aggressiveness depends on the level of testosterone in circulation (Montoya et al., 2012). This level can be increased, for example, with the consumption of steroids. Thus, people who abuse alcohol and take steroids and other drugs provoke an alteration in their brain chemistry. Low levels of serotonin, the neurotransmitter in charge of activating the "brakes" so that a person does not commit violent acts, and high testosterone levels is a terrible combination that can cause a person to display violent behaviors.

Genetic Factors

There have been reported cases in which violent actions have been shown to originate from certain genetic alterations in the person. In investigations conducted by Michelle Gotz and her team from the Psychiatry Department at the Royal Edinburgh Hospital in Great Britain, a variety of families in which there were various criminals were analyzed. The common feature between these families turned out to be an alteration in a gene that contributes to the production of an enzyme known as monoamine oxidase type A. This enzyme regulates the production of neurotransmitters such as serotonin and dopamine, which, as mentioned, are very important for the regulation of the emotional state (Mehta, Goetz, & Carré, 2013). People who have this kind of alteration experience continuous states of explosive aggression.

Other studies have shown that, in addition to this alteration, violent people often have a history of child abuse. In other words, simply having this genetic alteration meant individuals had a low tolerance to frustration and got angry easily; however, in violent killers, in addition to this alteration, there was a history of child abuse (Caspi et al., 2002). According to these findings, individuals who had explosive personalities, who were irritable, and who had a very low tolerance to frustration seldom only had the genetic alteration or experienced child abuse, but, when both factors (i.e. genetic and environmental) were present, dangerously violent personalities were generated, including killers and serial killers.

From a Darwinian evolutionary point of view, the social function of psychopathological personality could be speculated: maybe these people act as "insurance" for the species or social group during emergencies, because these personalities often have unusual reactions to totally anomalous, unforeseen, or strange situations. For example, in the battlefield, the one who is labeled as "soulless," "cruel," and "insensitive" turns out to be the hero. He is the one at the front, the one who takes more risks than the rest of the population, and the one who takes forward actions that most people would not dare to carry out—commanding a war platoon, for example. In this way, the psychopath would adjust perfectly to the emergency requirements of unnatural situations. In other words, from an evolutionary perspective, it could be speculated that psychopaths are part of the social reserve of reaction in certain situations. The anticipation of danger and fear does not inhibit them in taking action and they are, consequently, refractory to aversive conditions. However, that potential is completely unfavorable in times of peace, turning them into dangerous individuals for society.

Biology Is Not Everything

Not everything is determined by brain chemistry. There are certain psychopathic traits that can be observed from childhood, such as cruelty towards animals or other children, contempt for school hierarchies, or behavioral aberrations that are "softened" by teachers and family members with the pretext that we are talking about "emotional problems" or "mischief." In this context, a series of significant environmental factors have been identified. For example, some psychologists, such as Kenneth Levy from the Department of Psychology at the University of Pennsylvania, point out that psychopaths may have been raised by overprotective parents, with the child learning to expect to be treated by everyone in a special way and for all obstacles to what they want to be removed (Levy, 2005).

Other studies of serial killers have shown that they can be deprived or neglected children who develop a personality disorder as a protective mechanism to hide their low self-esteem. Conditions that could lead to a personality disorder are a lack of human comfort, neglect from parents that forces the child to depend upon themselves, and problems that affect the emotional attachment between the parents and the child, either as a result of harm to the child or through difficulties with the parents (Hickey, 2012). In this way, the child learns that the world is cold and loveless and that he or she lives in a vicious place. To protect him- or herself from this hostile world, he or she develops self-protection characteristics, such as aggressiveness, belligerent manners, deceit, resentment towards authority, or an ability to "turn on" and "turn off" charm. Ironically, these traits can repel other people and, therefore, the child's vision of the world as a hostile place is confirmed. The final result of this vicious circle is psychopathy.

In summary, it seems that, to develop a psychopathic personality in the strict sense of the concept, the simultaneous presence of several factors is necessary, such as certain inherited temperamental characteristics, deficiencies in brain function, a lack of control and emotional learning, experiences of abuse during childhood, and a parents–child relationship without attachment.

The Evaluation of Psychopathy

There is a long list of behaviors and symptoms that are associated with the possible presence of psychopathy. The most common measure of such behaviors and symptoms is the Hare Psychopathy Checklist, proposed by researcher Robert Hare (1999b), an expert in psychopathic personality. To apply this checklist, it is very important to remember that the presence of one of the traits does not mean that the person is a psychopath. A group of traits must be shown, as otherwise we would believe that we are surrounded by psychopaths. In addition, the traits must be persistent and not occasional. Their intensity and quality must be evaluated through behavior and affect in the environment.

In their actions, psychopaths do not always show evident traits of their disorder. For example, there are no physical characteristics that distinguish psychopaths; they are people just like everyone else. It is possible to recognize them only when they act in a psychopathic way. It must be said that they are not all brilliant and successful. There are those who are introverted and reclusive; others only show their true selves in private situations—for example, they appear to everyone, except to their partner, as an ordinary person. *Rethinking Risk Assessment: The MacArthur Study of Mental Disorder and Violence* (Monahan et al., 2001) points out that about 3% of men and 1% of women could be considered psychopaths. Taking this into account, in a country such as the United States, the population of psychopaths could be several millions of people.

It must be noted that there are several degrees of psychopathy; that is, there are some people who persistently show several traits that characterize them as psychopaths, while other people show only psychopathic tendencies—in other words, their personality includes only some abnormal traits.

The Hare Psychopathy Checklist, mentioned above, includes 20 items that are each scored on a points basis. The total number of points required for a psychopathic diagnosis is 30. Total points can vary from 0 to 40, and the points total reflects the degree to which the individual fits the psychopathic personality type. In the normal population, people's scores range from 0 to 15 points. In the population of prison inmates, the average score ranges from 22 to 24 and, in psychiatric hospitals, it varies between 18 and 20.

The items that are included in the checklist are outlined below and these are, consequently, considered distinctive psychopathic characteristics. The score for each item can be 0, 1, or 2 points. The points are assigned as follows: 2 points when the subject's behavior is consistent and fully matches the item in question; 1 point when the subject's behavior somewhat matches the item, but not to the degree required to score 2; and 0 points when the subject's behavior does not match the item at all—in other words, the subject does not show the trait or behavior in question.

1. *Superficial charm:* a tendency to be extremely verbal and assertive, without being afraid to say things, and a feeling of being free from social conventions, such as respecting turns when speaking. Not all psychopaths have a seductive

personality; there are also those who show no interest in others and who are bitter and harsh, and some of them others, frankly, find repulsive. There are even those who are extreme and inspire fear. The group that uses charm includes the more exploitative individuals (swindlers, bon vivants, social parasites), who do so as a method for acquisition (see Item 5, Cunning and manipulation).

2. *Grandiose (exaggeratedly high) estimation of self:* an immeasurable sense of one's own abilities and self-value. These people express their opinions in an incisive way. They are arrogant people who consider themselves superior to others.

3. *Need for stimulation:* a need for continuous stimulation. These people need novel, risky, and exciting challenges. They like challenges and carry out dangerous activities. They have poor self-discipline: they find it difficult to complete activities because they get bored easily. They fail when they try to keep their jobs for a long time or try to finish tasks that they consider routine.

4. *Pathological lying:* the use of lies as a tool. These people are manipulative, dishonest, and unscrupulous.

5. *Cunning and manipulation:* the deception of others for personal gain. This item is distinguishable from Item 4 because of the degree to which exploitation and rudeness are used here, reflected in a lack of interest in or worry about the feelings and suffering of others.

6. *Lack of remorse and guilt:* a lack of feelings for or worries about the loss, pain, and suffering of others. These people have a tendency to have little empathy and they are very cold.

7. *Shallow affects:* emotional poverty or a limited range of deep feelings, with coldness in interpersonal relationships in spite of signs of being gregarious.

8. *Callousness and lack of empathy:* feelings of indifference towards others, coldness, inconsiderateness, and insensitivity.

9. *Parasitic lifestyle:* intentional economic dependence, and being manipulative and selfish. This way of being is reflected in a constant lack of motivation, poor self-discipline, and a total inability to start or complete acquired responsibilities.

10. *Poor self-control:* expressions of irritability, lack of patience, threats, aggression and verbal abuse, and inadequate anger and temperament control.

11. *Sexual promiscuity:* superficial and short relationships, indiscriminate selection of sexual partners, having several relationships at the same time, a history of trying to force others during sexual activities, and/or showing off their about their sexual exploits.

12. *Early behavioral problems:* before the age of 13 years, behaviors such as lying, stealing, cheating, vandalism, disturbance, sexual activities, drug and alcohol abuse, and running away from home are seen.

13. *Lack of realistic long-term goals:* a nomadic existence.

14. *Impulsivity:* behaviors displayed without consideration or planning. These people have an inability to resist temptation, are easily frustrated, in emergencies act in a hurry and without considering the consequences, and display erratic behaviors without caution.

15. *Irresponsibility:* a continual inability to fulfill and value obligations and promises, such as not paying bills, doing jobs without care, being absent, arriving late for work, or not executing contracts.

16 *Failure to accept responsibility for actions:* this is reflected in a lack of compromise, antagonistic manipulation, denial of responsibility, and attempts to manipulate others through negotiations.

17. *Many short-term marital relationships:* a lack of compromise in relationships, reflected in inconsistent bonds, without dependence, and being untrustworthy.

18. *Juvenile delinquency:* behavior problems between the ages of 13 and 18 years, including crimes, antagonistic actions, exploitation, aggression, and manipulation.

19. *Revocation of conditional release:* conditional release from prison is revoked due to technical violations, such as not presenting themselves in court.

20. *Criminal versatility:* committing a variety of criminal offenses, and, when not arrested, being proud to "get away with it."

The points from these items are classified as follows:

- 0–20: normal;
- 21–29: psychopathic tendencies;
- 30 or more: psychopath.

In addition to the characteristics mentioned above, there are other personality traits that are often characteristic of a psychopath. For example:

- *Treating others as objects.* This trait consists in depriving other people of the traits that make them equal. A psychopath uses people, treating them as objects that are disposed of when they are no longer of use. This treating others as objects allows a psychopath to harm, kill, and torture others, because an object, unlike a person, can be eliminated and mistreated.

- *An ability to understand others' needs.* This is another important trait of psychopaths: seduction. A psychopath suggests to others that he or she needs them, but, at the same time, makes him- or herself much more necessary to them. In this way, a relationship is created between the psychopath and the other person to satisfy the psychopath's needs. If the psychopath's other characteristics, such as his or her potential to be intelligent and manipulative, are considered, we realize that it is very difficult for others to resist psychopaths.

Domestic Violence

In relationships where domestic violence occurs, there is often a codependency between the psychopathic abuser and the victim. This is because the psychopath undermines the self-esteem of the other, who finally comes to believe that the psychopath is right. This results in a common problem in clinical treatment: separating the psychopath from his or her partner is a very complex issue. The first thing you should do is help the person who is associated with the psychopath to raise his or her self-esteem and strengthen his or her own identity. Second, it is important for the victim to understand the personality of his or her partner and why he or she behaves in that way.

Disagreements are part of human relationships and they can often lead to aggression and anger. However, when that aggression becomes uncontrolled anger or violence, it can lead to mistreatment; that situation is abnormal, unhealthy, and obviously risky to physical and mental integrity. Verbal aggression, such as insults, and physical aggression, such as violence and mistreatment, as well as sexual abuse, are all intrinsically harmful. Threats and verbal, physical, and sexual abuse cause psychological and physical harm. It is often the case that the victim in an abusive relationship feels guilty and believes that he or she "deserves" mistreatment.

Physical abuse is considered to be when a person receives any kind of blow. Through these behaviors, the perpetrator tries to gain control over and dominate the person who is assaulted. Statistics show that thousands of people are seriously injured or killed by their peers, partners, or relatives (Heise, 1998).

Learned Behavior

Family violence is not a natural behavior, but a product of learning (Barnett, Miller-Perrin, & Perrin, 2010). When children live in a violent atmosphere, the likelihood that they will develop behavioral problems such as depression, anxiety, post-traumatic stress, poor school performance, and learned helplessness is increased. In other words, they learn that they cannot escape or avoid being attacked and that there are no positive expectations for the future (Osofsky, 1995, 1999).

It is common that such children feel frightened or ashamed or come to think that they caused the problem. In addition, children can grow up with the belief that it is right to hurt others or to let others hurt them. Often, people who are in abusive relationships are not sure of the degree of normality of their relationships, and do not question whether or not throwing objects, receiving insults, or verbal aggression are normal.

Legal and Therapeutic Challenges

The issue of psychopathy is also complicated in the legal and medical fields. Immediately when considering psychopathy, the question emerges of whether, through science, a solution or an effective treatment could be found. Although effective therapies are not yet available, training in cognitive skills has begun to be developed to encourage psychopaths to be empathetic to the thoughts and feelings of others in (Reid & Gacono, 2000; Seto & Barbaree, 1999). These therapies are based on the belief that a psychopath's behavior is born from a total inability to process emotions. However, it has been suggested that psychopaths can be trained and managed but not cured (Benn, 2014).

From a legal point of view, the decision about whether a psychopath is guilty and responsible is complex. Although these people are not mentally disordered, in the conventional sense, they do not have a good emotional balance. Therefore, although they should not be exempted from legal responsibility because of mental illness, it seems unfair to apply the same penalty to them as to a normal person, and it is also impossible to leave the decision with them about whether they will receive therapy or not.

A variety of therapeutic models have been suggested (Salekin, Worley, & Grimes, 2010). Therapy usually consists in providing cognitive training to allow psychopaths to understand the thoughts and feelings of other people, to broaden their worldview, and to help them to form new interpretations of social obligations and norms. It is necessary to teach them to understand the feelings of other people, helping these offenders to understand the ultimate reason for their way of being and their inability to feel the emotions of others.

According to Federico Lösel (1998), Professor of Psychology at the University of Erlangen, Germany, and a specialist in intervention programs, the most promising programs are the cognitive, behavioral, and structured programs that cover criminogenic needs and individual learning styles of offenders. For a relatively promising treatment program for psychopaths, Lösel suggests that the following principles must be considered:

1. *Use a solid conceptual and theoretical basis.* Start from what is empirically known about psychopathy and criminal behavior. Teach skills to promote self-control and reduce criminal behavior or alcohol abuse.
2. *Conduct a deep and dynamic assessment of the offender.* Evaluate the degree of motivation and crime thoroughly. Information related to the crime can help develop an understanding of the connection between the basic personality of the psychopath and the risk of recidivism.
3. *Follow an intensive treatment schedule.* Psychopaths need intensive and ongoing treatment, not short programs.
4. *Use institutions with clearly structured environments.* The institutional environment should avoid reinforcing manipulation, reproaches, negotiations, and other typical techniques of psychopaths. We must impose and enforce clear and strict responsibilities, regulations, rights, obligations, and rules. The rules should be established beforehand to avoid the traps that psychopaths use to manipulate others.
5. *Use cognitive–behavioral programs.* These are designed to change the cognitive distortions, denials, or mitigations that these people use to justify their actions. In cases that require it, drug treatment should be included to manage impulsivity.
6. *Use controlled monitoring and relapse prevention.* The treatment of antisocial behavior often has only superficial or temporary effects. It is necessary to assess if psychopaths are making use of the skills learned in treatment, and

evaluation should depend not only on what the subject says, but also on objective data, work files, and information from third parties.

7. *Provide support to families.* They need to understand the characteristics of psychopaths so they can identify and avoid the lies, manipulation, and deception that psychopaths use.

8. *Begin prevention and intervention at an early age.* In cold and insensitive children and those with behavioral disorders, it is important to intervene before these behaviors interact with other social factors and gradually get worse. Effective programs for children in risky situations should include elements that improve cognitive and social skills and reduce impulsivity and attention deficit, as well as elements that improve the behavior of parents. Programs that begin at an early age and that are multimodal and intensive seem to be very promising.

An Example: Roberto González Ruiz[1]

As an example of a psychopathic personality, we discuss the case of Roberto González Ruiz, a 35-year-old man who is currently serving 60 years in a prison in Mexico City for kidnapping and murder. In the highly dangerous module where he is, he consumes and sells drugs. He often violently attacks those who do not meet his expectations and his fellow prison inmates treat him with a mixture of fear and respect.

His criminal history began when he was 9 years old when he stole some equipment from his school. Just two years later, at the age of 11, he was stealing cars. He was often expelled from school because of challenging and assaulting teachers and prefects. He has said that, since he was a child, he liked to mistreat animals and one of his greatest amusements was burning cats and dogs, as he enjoyed watching them running on fire as if they were "fireballs."

The list of crimes that he has committed is long: theft of cardholders at banks and ATMs, kidnapping, torture, and murder. He has had several jobs, but none of them stable: he has stayed in most of them for only a week. In his mind, stealing was his profession. In interactions with him, he is a very friendly person and he often had "friends" in his gang, but because of fights between them and the consequent estrangement, he used to leave them and form new groups.

He has never married but has had several partners. The longest relationship he has had lasted three months and ended because of the violence between them. In prison, he is often visited by three different "girlfriends," although he describes himself as monogamous. He can recount, in detail, how he tortured and butchered the victims whom he kidnapped, whose families did not pay the ransom to free them. He has also said that he committed some of his murders because he was hired. He does not report feelings of guilt or shame in relation to any of these actions. When questioning him on this matter, he simply responds that "it was a job" and it was "his life or the other person's life" because, if he did not kill them, those who had hired him would kill him.

Roberto's behavior can be classified as antisocial personality disorder, manifested as a continuous pattern of rule breaking and violation of the rights of others, which started before he was 15 years old and has continued into adulthood. This criminal shows a lack of respect for social rules, impulsivity, aggression, and irresponsibility. However, in addition to his antisocial behavior, he shows emotional disturbance: he is charming and manipulative, he does not experience feelings of empathy or guilt, and he is unable to form enduring emotional bonds. In the Hare Psychopathy Checklist, Roberto gets a score of 36, a number that defines him as a psychopath.

Note

1 To protect the security of this individual and the author of this book, both the name and some of the personal information about the person involved have been modified.

References

American Academy of Pediatrics (2001). Shaken baby syndrome: Rotational cranial injuries: Technical report. *Pediatrics*, 108(1), 206–210.

American Psychiatric Association—Task Force on DSM-IV (1994). *Diagnostic and Statistical Manual Of Mental Disorders: DSM-IV*. Washington, DC: American Psychiatric Association.

American Psychiatric Association (2013). *DSM 5*. Washington, DC: American Psychiatric Association.

Barnett, O.W., Miller-Perrin, C.L., & Perrin, R.D. (2010). *Family Violence Across the Lifespan: An Introduction*. Thousand Oaks, CA: SAGE Publications.

Benn, S. (2014). Psychopathic criminals cannot be cured. *Psychology Today*, August. Retrieved on January 1, 2017 from: www.psychologytoday.com/blog/wicked-deeds/201408/psychopathic-criminals-cannot-be-cured.

Bismuth, N. (2010). *Are You Married to a Psychopath?* Toronto, Canada: McArthur & Co.

Caspi, A., McClay, J., Moffitt, T.E., Mill, J., Martin, J., Craig, I.W., ... & Poulton, R. (2002). Role of genotype in the cycle of violence in maltreated children. *Science*, 297(5582), 851–854.

Cleckley, H. (1941). *The Mask of Sanity: An Attempt to Reinterpret the So-Called Psychopathic Personality*. St. Louis, MO: C.V. Mosby Co.

Curtis, L. (2008). *Jack the Ripper and the London Press*. New Haven, CT: Yale University Press.

Dalley, J.W., & Roiser, J.P. (2012). Dopamine, serotonin and impulsivity. *Neuroscience*, 215, 42–58.

Decety, J., Chen, C., Harenski, C., & Kiehl, K.A. (2013). An fMRI study of affective perspective taking in individuals with psychopathy: Imagining another in pain does not evoke empathy. *Frontiers in Human Neuroscience*, 7: 489.

Encyclopaedia Britannica (n.d.). Luis Garavito. Retrieved on January 1, 2017 from: www.britannica.com/biography/Luis-Garavito.

Hare, R.D. (1996). Psychopathy and antisocial personality disorder: A case of diagnostic confusion. *Psychiatric Times*, 13(2), 39–40.

Hare, R.D. (1999a). Psychopathy as a risk factor for violence. *Psychiatric Quarterly*, 70(3), 181–197.

Hare, R.D. (1999b). *The Hare Psychopathy Checklist-Revised: PCL-R*. North Tonawanda, NY: MHS, Multi-Health Systems.

Hare, R.D., & Neumann, C.S. (2009). *Psychopathy*. New York, NY: Oxford University Press.

Heise, L.L. (1998). Violence against women: An integrated, ecological framework. *Violence Against Women*, 4(3), 262–290.

Hickey, E.W. (2012). *Serial Murderers and Their Victims*. Boston, MA: Cengage Learning.

Levy, K.N. (2005). The implications of attachment theory and research for understanding borderline personality disorder. *Development and Psychopathology*, 17(4), 959–986.

Lilienfeld, S.O. (2011). Psychopathic personality: Bridging the gap between scientific evidence and public policy. *Psychological Science in the Public Interest*, 12(3), 95–162.

Lösel, F. (1998). Treatment and management of psychopaths. In: Cooke, D.J., Forth, A.E., & Hare, R.D. (eds), *Psychopathy: Theory, Research and Implications for Society*. Amsterdam: Springer Netherlands. pp. 303–354.

Mazur, A. (2006). The role of testosterone in male dominance contests that turn violent. *Biodemography and Social Biology*, 53(1–2), 24–29.

Mazur, A. (2008). Testosterone and violence among young men. In: Walsh, A., & Beaver, K.M. (eds), *Biosocial Criminology*. New York, NY: Routledge. pp. 190–204.

McCord, J. (2007). *Crime and Family: Selected Essays of Joan McCord*. Philadelphia, PA: Temple University Press.

Mehta, P.H., Goetz, S.M., & Carré, J.M. (2013). Genetic, hormonal, and neural underpinnings of human aggressive behavior. In: Franks, D.D., & Turner, J.H. (eds), *Handbook of Neurosociology*. Amsterdam: Springer Netherlands. pp. 47–65.

Millon, T., & Davis, R.O. (1996). *Disorders of Personality: DSM-IV and Beyond*. Hoboken, NJ: John Wiley & Sons.

Monahan, J., Steadman, H.J., Silver, E., Appelbaum, P.S., Robbins, P.C., Mulvey, E.P., … & Banks, S. (2001). *Rethinking Risk Assessment: The MacArthur Study of Mental Disorder and Violence*. Oxford, UK: Oxford University Press.

Montoya, E.R., Terburg, D., Bos, P.A., & Van Honk, J. (2012). Testosterone, cortisol, and serotonin as key regulators of social aggression: A review and theoretical perspective. *Motivation and Emotion*, 36(1), 65–73.

Osofsky, J.D. (1995). The effect of exposure to violence on young children. *American Psychologist*, 50(9), 782.

Osofsky, J.D. (1999). The impact of violence on children. *The Future of Children*, 9(3), 33–49.

Patrick, C.J. (ed.). (2005). *Handbook of Psychopathy*. New York, NY: Guilford Press.

Patrick, C.J., & Bernat, E.M. (2009). From markers to mechanisms: Using psychophysiological measures to elucidate basic processes underlying aggressive externalizing behavior. In: Hodgins, S., Viding, E., & Plodowski, A. (eds), *Persistent Violent Offenders: Neuroscience and Rehabilitation*. London: Oxford University Press. pp. 223–250.

Patrick, C.J., & Berthot, B.D. (1995). Startle potentiation during anticipation of a noxious stimulus: Active versus passive response sets. *Psychophysiology*, 32(1), 72–80.

Patrick, C.J., & Zempolich, K.A. (1999). Emotion and aggression in the psychopathic personality. *Aggression and Violent Behavior*, 3(4), 303–338.

Patrick, C.J., Bradley, M.M., & Lang, P.J. (1993). Emotion in the criminal psychopath: Startle reflex modulation. *Journal of Abnormal Psychology*, 102(1), 82.

Patrick, C.J., Cuthbert, B.N., & Lang, P.J. (1994). Emotion in the criminal psychopath: Fear image processing. *Journal of Abnormal Psychology*, 103(3), 523.

Pinel, P. (1806). *A Treatise on Insanity*. Sheffield, UK: W. Todd.

Prichard, J.C. (1837). *A Treatise on Insanity: And Other Disorders Affecting the Mind* (Vol. 1837). Philadelphia, PA: Haswell, Barrington, and Haswell.

Raine, A., & Yang, Y. (2006). The neuroanatomical bases of psychopathy. In: Patrick, C.J. (ed.), *Handbook of Psychopathy*. New York, NY: Guilford Press. pp. 278–295.

Raine, A., Meloy, J.R., Bihrle, S., Stoddard, J., LaCasse, L., & Buchsbaum, M.S. (1998). Reduced prefrontal and increased subcortical brain functioning assessed using positron emission tomography in predatory and affective murderers. *Behavioral Sciences & the Law*, 16(3), 319–332.

Reid, W.H., & Gacono, C. (2000). Treatment of antisocial personality, psychopathy, and other characterologic antisocial syndromes. *Behavioral Sciences & the Law*, 18(5), 647–662.

Salekin, R.T., Worley, C., & Grimes, R.D. (2010). Treatment of psychopathy: A review and brief introduction to the mental model approach for psychopathy. *Behavioral Sciences & the Law*, 28(2), 235–266.

Semple, D., & Smyth, R. (eds). (2013). *Oxford Handbook of Psychiatry*. New York, NY: Oxford University Press.

Seto, M.C., & Barbaree, H.E. (1999). Psychopathy, treatment behavior, and sex offender recidivism. *Journal of Interpersonal Violence*, 14(12), 1235–1248.

Thompson, D.F., Ramos, C.L., & Willett, J.K. (2014). Psychopathy: Clinical features, developmental basis and therapeutic challenges. *Journal of Clinical Pharmacy and Therapeutics*, 39(5), 485–495.

Yang, Y., & Raine, A. (2009). Prefrontal structural and functional brain imaging findings in antisocial, violent, and psychopathic individuals: A meta-analysis. *Psychiatry Research: Neuroimaging*, 174(2), 81–88.

5

SERIAL KILLERS

Introduction

Criminology defines a serial killer as an individual who shows the following characteristics: kills on at least three occasions and with a certain time span between each murder; establishes direct contact with the victim; uses a knife, strangles, or strikes, and seldom uses a firearm; and, finally, commits the crime as a sort of ritual in which he or she is stimulated, combining personal fantasies with death (Kraemer, Lord, & Heilbrun, 2004).

It is generally believed that serial killers show specific social and psychological characteristics, such as an antisocial personality (Hare, 1999), a history of abuse during childhood (Beasley, 2004), and, frequently, traits of sexual sadism (Warren, Hazelwood, & Dietz, 1996). However, there is important variability among serial killers, related not only to personal background and sexual interests, but also to age, history of alcohol and other substance abuse, cultural level, sex, specific circumstances surrounding the crimes, and the victims' characteristics (Ardila & Ostrosky-Solís, 2009). Serial killers tend to be young people—sometimes even children and teenagers (Myers, 2004), and few cases of serial killers have been those in middle age. An extremely uneven distribution in sex is also observed: despite the fact that the significant majority of serial killers are men, this type of crime is also committed, but at a much smaller frequency, by women (Ostrosky-Solís et al., 2008; Wilson & Hilton, 1998). Taking all previously known information into account, the typical serial killer is a young man aged between 25 and 35 years (Beasley, 2004; Godwin, 2008; Hickey, 2012; Kraemer, Lord, & Heilbrun, 2004).

The psychopathic killer, who is a classic example of antisocial personality, can be classified as the most dangerous type of murderer, because this type of killer has the ability to fake emotions that he or she does not really feel. This trait allows the killer to develop an image of him- or herself to deceive the victim and to physically approach them, which will finally allow the killer to commit the murder. Psychopathic serial killers constantly try to gratify their own pleasure, they are lonely, and they frequently have a seductive personality (Angrilli, Sartori, & Donzella, 2013; Egger, 2002; Wilson & Seaman, 2007).

These criminals believe that they should be allowed to do anything and they get excited by forbidden and risky situations. When they kill, their final objective tends to be to humiliate their victim and, in this way, to experience power, regain authority, and reinforce their self-esteem. For these people, criminal activity is secondary; their main intention is to satisfy a keen desire for domination and superiority.

Who Are They?

There are three firm ideas that rule serial killers' minds: manipulation, domination, and control of the situation. However, given their way of acting when they commit their crimes, according to the Federal Bureau of Investigation of the United States of America (FBI), it is possible to classify them into two main categories (Douglas et al., 2013).

The first of these is the *organized killer*. Organized killers are methodic people who carefully plan their crimes, stalk their prey, carry with them their preferred and distinctive weapon, and, only then, once they have the victim in their power, do they proceed to commit the crime slowly and sadistically. Their main characteristics are:

- has an above-average IQ;
- is socially adequate;
- lives with a partner or dates frequently;
- has/had an unstable father figure;
- has experienced physical abuse within the family—that is, a harsh environment;
- is geographically/occupationally mobile;
- follows the news;
- may be college educated;
- has good hygiene/housekeeping skills;
- does not usually have a hiding place;
- has diurnal (daytime) habits;
- needs to return to the crime scene to see what the police authorities have done;
- usually contacts the police to play games;
- kills at one site, disposes at another;
- may dismember the body;
- attacks using seduction and then gets the victim into restraints;
- is social and capable of holding a conversation;

- leaves a controlled crime scene;
- leaves little physical evidence;
- responds best to direct interview.

The second category of serial killers is the *disorganized killer*. Disorganized killers, who are dominated by sudden impulse, choose their victims spontaneously, restrain them, and kill with any weapon or object that is to hand at that moment. Their main characteristics are:

- has a below-average IQ;
- is socially inadequate;
- lives alone and usually does not date;
- has/had an absent or unstable father;
- has experienced emotional abuse within the family, but this is inconsistent;
- lives and/or works near the crime scene;
- has minimal interest in the news;
- is usually a high-school dropout;
- has poor hygiene/housekeeping skills;
- has a secret hiding place in the home;
- has nocturnal (nighttime) habits;
- needs to return to the crime scene to relive memories;
- may contact the victim's family to play games;
- has no interest in police work;
- kills at one site and considers the mission over;
- usually leaves the body intact;
- attacks in a "blitz" pattern;
- depersonalizes the victim as an inanimate object;
- leaves a chaotic crime scene;
- leaves physical evidence;
- responds best to counseling interview.

Candice Skrapec, a criminologist at California State University, Fresno, has pointed out that one characteristic of serial killers is that they act following their own original logic, which is almost always different from common sense (Skrapec, 2001). Another trait that is common in these personalities, and contrary to popular belief, is that these people (or organized killers, at least) possess an IQ superior to the average, combined with dexterity and a special ability to appear as "normal" as any other person. These features are presented as the main reason why, often, the police authorities have great difficulties tracking them down. There are many cases in which, for years, serial killers have evaded their pursuers, leaving behind them a trail of corpses without any clue about their identities.

The Profile of a Serial Killer

Despite the fact that there have been many high-profile cases, television shows, and big movie productions about serial killers, there have actually been few published scientific and psychosocial studies that describe the characteristics of these individuals clearly. One of the most revealing studies was conducted by the researchers of the Psychology Department at the University of Philadelphia and their collaborators at the FBI (Kraemer, Lord, & Heilbrun, 2004), who compared the crimes committed by serial killers against those committed by sole killers. To carry out their investigation, they used a large database of serial killers' profiles. The study comprised 157 offenders and 608 victims. From the data, typical characteristics of serial killers and their victims can be seen, and these are given in Tables 5.1 and 5.2, respectively.

This information largely matches the US Department of Justice's statistics (Egger, 2002), which show that between 85% and 90% of serial killers are male, young, and in good physical shape.

TABLE 5.1 Characteristics of serial killers (adapted from Kraemer, Lord, & Heilbrun, 2004)

Prevailing gender: 95% male

Ethnic origin: 68% Caucasian

Average age: 31 years old

High-school level of education: 11.51 years

Marital status at the moment of committing the crime: 31% married, 16% previously married

Crime motive: 54% sexual, 24% emotional, 18% economic, 4% psychotic crisis of the killer

TABLE 5.2 Characteristics of serial killers' victims (adapted from Kraemer, Lord, & Heilbrun, 2004)

Prevailing gender: 67% female

Ethnic origin: 71% Caucasian

Average age: 33 years old

Relationship with the killer: 57% none, 21% acquaintances, 5% family members, 17% not clarified

Female Serial Killers

Female serial killers are considered particularly unusual (Frei et al., 2006; Kelleher & Kelleher, 1998). In recent times, there have been two well-known cases of female serial killers. The first, the American Aileen Wuornos (Reynolds, 2004; Wuornos, 2006), will be described later, and the second, Juana Barraza Samperio (Ostrosky-Solís et al., 2008), is probably the most famous Mexican female serial killer since the so-called Poquianchis (Holmes & Stephen, 1998).

Both of these serial killers, who were cold and calculative, shared the fact of having experienced a childhood with a lack of affection. What happens to the personality of a female child who lives in this way? The need for affection is as critical as the need for material support in a child and, when this need is unfulfilled, the child succumbs to feelings of anger, despair, and helplessness, and so, to be able to survive, she learns to separate or isolate her emotions. These emotional conflicts will be triggered during adulthood, when behaviors are no longer adaptive, which prevents these kinds of people from establishing permanent affectionate relationships.

Women also have more of a tendency than men to make attempts against their own families, according to the reports of the FBI and the US Department of Justice (Egger, 2002; Kraemer, Lord, & Heilbrun, 2004). These crimes committed by women against their families are often much less violent than the crimes of men, and women very rarely commit a homicide for sexual reasons.

A professor from the University of Valencia in Spain, José Sanmartín, who is also the author of the book *La Violencia y Sus Claves* (*Violence and Its Clues*; Sanmartín, 2013), claims that a common characteristic in homicides committed by women is that they do not tend to use firearms and they kill at knifepoint only very rarely. In fact, Sanmartín states that women choose more discreet and simple methods (such as poisoning or asphyxiation) than men, they tend to be very methodic and careful, they plan the crime meticulously and in a very subtle way to make it more difficult for the investigators who try to hunt them, and, on more than one occasion, they have been ignored by the press, since many people believe that a female serial killer is no more than a woman who suffers from schizophrenia or another mental disorder.

However, studies reported by Jürgen Thorwald in his book *Die Stunde der Detektive* (*The Century of Criminal Investigation*; translated by Feliu Formosa to Spanish; Thorwald & Formosa, 1966) and by Gerald Godwin in *Hunting Serial Predators* (Goodwin, 2008) about the psychological profile of female serial killers have shown that these kinds of killers have psychopathic personalities and truly criminal minds. Studies seem to agree that most female serial killers develop this disorder in early childhood, generally marked by traumatic episodes and unfavorable life conditions.

The Development of a Serial Killer

The typical serial killer follows a progressive model of development that begins with fantasy and ends in depression. This structure has been described by one of the key American experts in this subject, Joel Norris, in his book *Serial Killers* (Norris, 1988):

- *Aura phase.* This phase comes before the process of killing. It is the point in the potential killer's life in which he or she begins to lock him- or herself up in an imaginary world; externally, the person seems normal, but inside his or her head is a dark place where the idea of a crime starts to develop and he or she fantasizes about it. The person's contact with reality is weakened and his or her mind starts to be dominated by daydreams of death and destruction. Gradually, the need to free these fantasies becomes a compulsion.
- *Trolling phase.* Just like a fisherman searching lakes and rivers for the best fishing spot, the killer starts his or her search in those places where he or she considers the "precise type" of victim can be found. A school's playground, a red-light district, or a town might be chosen. Once the ideal site is found, it is established as his or her target.
- *Wooing phase.* In some cases, the serial killer attacks without warning, often capturing a victim from the street or breaking into a house. However, he or she can feel a particular pleasure in attracting victims by generating a false feeling of security and circumventing their defenses. Some serial killers are so alluring and have such a harmless appearance that they do not find it difficult to convince a person to get inside their car, lure a child by offering sweets, or seduce people with the promise of giving them money, work, or a place to spend the night.
- *Capture phase.* This is the closing of the trap. At the moment that these killers have the opportunity to see the terrified reactions of their victims, a sort of sadistic game begins, which they generally enjoy immensely. This happens, for example, when a woman who has gotten inside the car of this "kind stranger" finds out that he or she is driving in the wrong direction and that the passenger door does not have a handle.
- *Murder phase.* In many cases, the act of committing the crime can be a substitute for a sexual act; that is, the moment when the victim finally dies represents the climax that the serial killer was looking for and had needed since the moment when the fantasies of committing the murder began. For this reason, it is not strange that many psychopaths feel a real orgasm at the moment they kill. Serial killers also often have a preference for one particular homicidal technique; therefore, some of them enjoy strangling, whereas others enjoy beating or stabbing.
- *Totem phase.* Just like in someone with paraphilia, the murder allows these people to feel an intense but transitory pleasure. To prolong the experience during the period before the next murder, the killer keeps a trophy associated with the victim, such as a wallet, a photograph, or even a piece of the body.

- *Depression phase.* After the crime, the serial killer experiences a depressive phase, which could be compared to post-coital sadness. This crisis can be so deep that he or she might try to commit suicide. However, the most common reaction to this feeling is translated into a renewed desire to commit homicide.

The Stages of a Serial Killer's Operation

Specialist José Sanmartín (Sanmartín, 2013) describes three stages of a serial killer's operation:

1. *Before the murder.* Psychotic killers act under what they consider orders from superior entities, such as God or Satan. These types of killers do not plan their crimes and, therefore, do not choose their victims logically: they often attack the first person they see/encounter. By contrast, the psychopathic serial killer, or at least the organized killer subgroup, commits his or her crime with clear judgment and plans it in detail: he or she knows what he or she is going to do and does not want to fail. This type of killer is often controlled and obsessed with abhorrent fantasies, which he or she may have been recreating in his or her imagination since childhood or puberty, and these guide him or her in choosing the victim: for example, "young women with long straight hair, parted in the middle." However, it is not only anatomical characteristics but also psychological traits such as meekness that attract killers. As Sanmartín points out, to remove the victim's absolute control is one of the recurring objectives of organized killers.
2. *During the murder.* The performance of the fantasy tends to require the use of certain instruments or tools. Because of this, it is not strange for the organized killer to carry instruments with him or her; in other words, a series of tools that he or she uses to kill, such as ropes, handcuffs, surgical knives, etc. By contrast, the disorganized killer uses whatever is at hand: for example, if he or she finds a knife at the victim's house, it can be used to stab the victim in the chest and it can then be left there. This represents another distinctive trait of disorganized killers: most of the time, they do not worry about removing their fingerprints, hiding the corpse, or taking other measures to make the criminal investigation complicated. By contrast, the organized killer plans his or her escape carefully and takes care not to leave signs that make his or her capture easy.
3. *After the murder.* After committing the crime, it is common for the organized killer to take a memento from the victim. These killers collect underwear, necklaces, shoes, and even body parts. These are "trophies" with which they may decorate their favorite room or add to a macabre collection.

Afterwards, a new cycle can begin, although the duration of the intervals between cycles may vary.

The Etiology of the Serial Killer

Studies conducted by Robert Ressler (Ressler, 1993, 1998; Douglas et al., 2013), an FBI expert in serial homicides, and Candice Skrapec (Skrapec, 2001), who has personally analyzed and interviewed a great number of serial killers of both genders, have given information about the causes of this personality disorder and the reasons why these people attack society in this way. Their investigations highlight that the search for excitement, dissociation, and a feeling of greatness are relevant factors in this phenomenon, along with the effects of a socialization process filled with abuse and violence.

Ressler and Skrapec both work on the theory that there are several environmental and social factors that can influence the development of a psychopathic personality. These are evidenced by the following:

- Approximately 60% of psychopaths have lost one of their parents.
- As children, psychopaths are often deprived of maternal love: parents are generally absent or distant.
- In psychopaths' history, there is often an improper disciplinary system, such as a ruthless father and a weak mother. In this way, the child learns to hate authority and manipulate the mother figure.
- Psychopaths often have dysfunctional parents who mistreat the child in private, while in society take care to project the image of a "happy family."
- The mother–child relationship plays a key role in the development of aggression and extreme violence. In other words, the more the child's upbringing is comprehensive and communicative, the less aggressive the child will be. By contrast, those mothers who openly show the frustration and anger that their children "cause them" and who often repeat to them that they are a burden tend to have very aggressive children.

There are other situations and factors that can lead to the development of homicidal psychopathic personalities. For example, future serial killers' relationships with their mothers tend to be marked by coldness, distance, and abandonment, and also by the absence of emotional warmth and body contact. In the same way, a violent or indifferent mother and a lack of attention from the father can be an explosive cocktail.

It has been proven that children who witness aggressive behavior towards their mothers usually develop feelings of pity, more than hatred, but a child who suffers abuse from the mother can become an aggressive adult with personality disorders, and even a psychopath. Most serial killers have been deeply mistreated and hurt during their childhood.

Famous Serial Killers

Because of the characteristics of their crimes, serial killers have been famous throughout history. The following are some of the most sadistic killers of all time:

- *Erszebet Bathory*, Hungary, committed approximately 600 crimes. Born as part of the Hungarian nobility, Bathory began to kill women in 1600, bleeding them and, "to recover her lost beauty," using their blood as a skin elixir (Thorne, 1997). When her passion for blood turned her towards noble young women, the authorities stopped her practices. Sentence: locked up in her own chambers in 1611 and died in 1614.

- *Pedro Alonso López*, Colombia, committed 300 crimes (100 proven). Between 1978 and 1980, Alonso raped and strangled dozens of girls and teens in Ecuador, Peru, and Colombia. After a failed kidnap in the city of Ambato, he was captured and forced to confess (Boar & Blundell, 1983). Sentence: life imprisonment, which he is currently serving in a prison in Ecuador.

- *H. H. Holmes*, USA, committed approximately 150 crimes. In 1893, Holmes, who had made a fortune committing fraud against insurance companies, took advantage of the World Fair in Chicago to build a guest house full of contraptions such as gas chambers, crematoriums, and secret passages, which he used to murder and mutilate 150 women who rented rooms in his establishment (Geary, 2003). Sentence: executed in May 1896.

- *Andrei Chikatilo*, Ukraine, committed approximately 50 crimes. Apparently traumatized by the circumstances in which he lived, between 1980 and 1992, Chikatilo killed, mutilated, and devoured prostitutes and abandoned children in forests and outside railway stations in the Ukrainian region of Rostov (Krivich & Olgin, 1993). Sentence: executed in February 1994.

- *Ahmad Suradji*, Indonesia, committed 42 crimes. Claiming to have magical powers, Suradji killed tens of women who were looking for magical protection in rituals performed on the outskirts of the Indonesian city of Medan, which ended with their deaths, between 1987 and 1997. Sentence: executed in April 1998.

- *Gerald Stano*, USA, committed 41 crimes. Apparently full of hatred towards women, Stano killed 41 women, but without raping them, during the 1980s, almost always stabbing them while giving them a ride in his car on highways in Florida, New Jersey, and Pennsylvania (Flowers, 1993; Kelly & Montane, 2011). Sentence: executed in March 1998.

- *Richard Kuklinski*, USA, committed approximately 40 crimes. Trained as a killer for the New York Mafia Gambino family, in 1980, Kuklinski used methods such as poisoning to kill on request and eliminate those who owed him money, or those who he simply did not like (Carlo, 2006). Sentence: double life imprisonment in Trenton State Prison in New Jersey; he died at the age of 70 on March 5, 2006.

- *Moses Sithole*, South Africa, committed 41 crimes. Between 1987 and 1995, Sithole tricked young women, offering them jobs, raping the most beautiful, and strangling them all. All this happened in the regions of Pretoria, Johannesburg, and East Rand (Newton, 2000). Sentence: 2,410 years in prison, which he is currently serving in Pretoria Central Prison.

- *John Wayne Gacy*, USA, committed 33 crimes. Gacy (a family man, businessman, and volunteer in community projects) began in 1976 a series of murders of male teens, whom he tied up, raped, and then beat to death. It ended in 1978 with his apprehension in Chicago (Linedecker, 1993). Sentence: executed in May 1994.
- *Jane Toppan*, USA, committed approximately 31 crimes. Between 1880 and 1901, this nurse killed tens of people (generally old and sick people) in the state of New England using overdoses of drugs such as morphine (Segrave, 1992). Sentence: declared mentally incompetent; she died in 1938 in a psychiatric hospital due to natural causes.

The Case of Aileen Wuornos

Aileen Wuornos represents one of the most complex stories of a serial killer (Hickey, 2012; Reynolds, 2004; Russell, 2002; Wuornos, 2006). She was born in 1956 and was the daughter of a child abuser—he committed suicide in prison—and of a woman who left her with her grandparents when she was a few months old. Wuornos had problems from an early age and, at the age of 14, she became pregnant.

After giving her child up for adoption, Wuornos started her life as a prostitute for truck drivers on the highways of Florida, a situation that only came to a pause when she was 21, when she got married to a man named Lewis Fell, but the marriage lasted only a few months. After that, her life consisted of prostitution and other offenses such as armed robbery, exhibitionism, and drug and alcohol abuse. In 1986, she met a woman named Tyria Moore with whom she fell in love, and they started a life together as a couple. But things started to go wrong quickly. Because Wuornos provided their only stable income working as a prostitute, they found themselves living in cheap motels. In December 1989, the owner of a repair shop of electronic devices was found dead on a highway near the town of Daytona in Florida. Months later, between June and July 1990, another five corpses were found inside their cars by the police. All of them were naked or semi-naked, without money, and had been shot by a .22 caliber gun.

This series of murders continued until a motor crash in which the couple in one of the cars involved aroused police suspicions. Some phone calls between Moore and Wuornos provided enough incriminating evidence to arrest the latter. The trial, as tends to happen in the United States, received much attention from the media, and it became even bigger when Arlene Pralle appeared on the scene. Pralle was a wealthy woman and took Wuornos' defense because, according to her, God had personally ordered her to defend the woman. Pralle even legally adopted Wuornos as her daughter.

However, none of this helped Wuornos, and in spite of her retelling her life story and the argument that she had committed the murders in self-defense, the evidence (including a videotaped confession) and Moore's testimony finally led to her conviction and, on January 27, 1992, she was sentenced to death in the electric chair.

In addition, Wuornos was put on trial for other offenses, of which she was declared guilty. During those trials, she continuously surprised, appearing brave, which distinguished her from other convicts who face the American penal system: she did not file the paperwork for the suspension of her execution and, in fact, asked to be executed voluntarily. She was executed on October 9, 2002 with a lethal injection.

In spite of everything, the motive of her crimes was never clear. Despite her problematic life, Wuornos did not commit any crimes until many years after she started her life as a prostitute, and robbery does not explain the undressing of the corpses or other characteristics of the crimes. It could be assumed that, after a life of abandonment, her relationship with Moore would have become the top priority of her life. Because of this, when economic problems threatened their relationship, Wuornos may have taken the easy path of robbery and murder, probably as an emotional escape from the threat of abandonment. But we will never know for sure.

This case received so much publicity and caused so much interest that there was even a movie about Wuornos. In 2003, the movie *Monster* was released. It starred Charlize Theron and Christina Ricci, and depicted the life and crimes of Wuornos.

The Case of Luis Alfredo Garavito

In 1999, Luis Alfredo Garavito challenged the stereotype of the intellectual, methodic, and cultivated serial killer with refined taste, who was typically embodied in Hannibal Lecter. Garavito committed hundreds of crimes without anyone noticing. Although he was arrested in April 1999 near the Colombian city of Villavicencio after trying to rape a minor, and although he confessed to having killed hundreds of children, police authorities did not believe him. They only took it seriously once one of his relatives showed them a box that contained the photographs he had taken from his victims' identification and a calendar where he marked the dates of his murders, which were committed in the regions of Tunja, Armenia, and Pereira.

Garavito's macabre operation was surprisingly simple: by pretending to be a street vendor, a cattle carrier, a peasant, a representative of an organization for helpless people, or a street trader, he used to deceive helpless children between 11 and 13 years of age who were near markets, promising them money or jobs. After taking them to faraway cropping fields, Garavito tortured them, raped them, cut their throats, and mutilated them (sometimes cutting their testicles or dismembering them), finally burying them without digging too deep.

Garavito committed the murders after drinking too much alcohol. In the case of this active serial killer, the psychological tests showed that he possessed below-average intelligence. In respect of the motive for his criminal behavior, a glimpse into his past provided disturbing evidence: he was beaten by his father and abused by his neighbors during his childhood. Since he was a child, he had wandered rural Colombia, which was shaken by armed violence. Diagnosed with a pattern of antisocial behavior and personality disorders, this man was able to lead a double life; he had lived for some time with women, some of whom even had children, on whom he had never laid a hand. But the question remains: how is it possible that a man, who was intellectually limited, could kill hundreds of people between 1992 and 1999, escaping from justice for a long time?

In spite of everything, this killer had good luck. Even nature was on his side: in 1999, an earthquake hit the city of Armenia in which criminal records, which could have been used in the investigations of the murders, were destroyed. As if this was not enough, because of his confession, the Colombian legal system exempted him from an open trial, although he was sentenced to more than 2,600 years in prison as a result of his 160 murders. However, because he has behaved very well in prison and because the Colombian Criminal Code forbids sentences of longer than 40 years in prison, it is likely that he will become a candidate for prerelease in this decade.

JB: From Victim to Multiple Homicide

This case of a middle-aged woman displays some remarkable characteristics: (1) in spite of the offender's harsh living conditions and traumatic childhood, there was no background of personality disorders when she began her serial killings; (2) personality testing did not reveal any evidence of psychiatric impairment; and (3) electrophysiological measures revealed alterations in her affective processing and a dissociation between her knowledge of how to behave in socially acceptable ways and her actual behavior (Ostrosky-Solís et al., 2008).

JB is a 48-year-old woman, born in Pachuca de Soto (in the state of Hidalgo, Mexico). Her family moved to Mexico City when she was three months old. Her father abandoned the family when she was born and her mother went to live with another man. JB has one half-brother and one half-sister. Her mother worked as a housemaid and was a heavy alcohol-abuser; her step-father worked as a handyman. The family was extremely poor and lived in a small, unfurnished house. JB took care of her two younger half-siblings, never attended school, and was not allowed to go out. She never had toys or friends to play with, and her mother was extremely aggressive (both physically and verbally) towards her. In general, JB's step-father was more protective towards her than her own mother. JB reported that, when she was about 12 years old, she was given away to an unfamiliar man (reportedly, her mother traded her for three bottles of beer). Allegedly, during their first night, JB was tied up and raped. She continued living with this man for 15 months in an abusive relationship, in which she was repeatedly raped. She later had a son outside this relationship. Soon after, JB was found by her step-uncle, who took her and her baby back to her family. JB said that her interaction with her mother was minimal, despite them living in the same house.

However, she maintained a good relationship with her step-father, who continued caring for JB and her son until his death, when she turned 30.

She reported no history of alcohol or drug abuse. JB worked for some time selling candy on the streets when she was approximately 12 years old, and later on in a shoe store. She married when she was 28 years old. Her husband was initially "a good man," as she declared, but he became progressively abusive (both physically and psychologically) towards her. JB had a daughter with this man when she was approximately 30 years of age, and left him three years later. At 34 years of age, she went to live with another man and had two more children. As with her first husband, they initially had a harmonious relationship, but he progressively became verbally and physically abusive towards her. At 45, she abandoned her partner and decided to live independently with her two younger children because her older daughter was married and her eldest son was killed in a street fight when he was 24 years old (JB was 38 at the time of his death). JB raised all of her three children, supporting her family by working on the streets selling candy and washing other people's clothing.

JB lived around the corner from a wrestling arena and, given her height, a trainer asked her if she wanted to be a wrestler (JB is relatively tall for a Mexican woman, about 5 feet 11 inches). JB decided to work in the professional wrestling business on weekends to make some extra money. Her wrestling name was "La Dama del Silencio" ("The Silent Lady"). When asked why this was her nickname, she responded "I have always been a quiet person, and I only speak when spoken to." Furthermore, JB pointed out that, when she was a wrestler, she belonged to the "rough or rude team and not the technical group because," according to her, "the rude follow rules during competition, as opposed to the technical." When she turned 43, after 13 years in wrestling, JB stopped participating as a wrestler and began working as an organizer of wrestling competitions. Before her current incarceration, she had no criminal record, although witnesses have accused her of breaking and entering.

JB is accused of killing at least 12 elderly women and attempting to kill another victim. According to police reports, at least six of the murders were associated with burglary. JB is known to the police and to the mass media as the *Mataviejitas* ("the killer of elderly women"). Initially, she confessed and described three of the crimes; however, in her trial, she pled guilty to only the final one, when she was caught committing the murder. The first murder attributed to the *Mataviejitas* was on November 17, 2003. The authorities and the press have given various estimates of the total number of the killer's victims, with totals ranging from 24 to 49 deaths.

The final killing was committed on January 25, 2006. According to the offender's report, JB approached an 82-year-old woman outside her home and asked if she would hire her as a laundry lady. Once in the house, the aged woman offered to pay an amount of money that JB considered too low: 23 pesos per 12 laundry pieces (approximately US$2). She asked for a higher payment and the lady answered in an insulting way: "These bitches, they're illiterate, but still want to make a lot of money!" JB killed her with the rubber cord of a stethoscope that was on the victim's table. JB was caught when a young man who was renting a room in the old woman's house came in unexpectedly. She tried to run away, but the young man chased her and two policemen managed to arrest her.

During the initial interrogation, JB admitted to killing another old lady around three years before. Reportedly, she met the old woman on the street; they talked for about an hour and a half, and JB escorted the old woman to her home. Once inside, JB asked her for a job. The lady purportedly responded that she was not used to having poor, dirty people in her house. JB responded that it was not fair to be judged in that manner, and strangled the lady with a stocking. She was accused of taking 4,000 pesos (approximately US$380) that she found at the lady's house. JB also declared that, about a year prior to her arrest, she met another aged woman, for whom she used to work doing laundry by hand. JB used to call this lady "Grandma." At some point during her working relationship, JB had no money and asked if she could borrow money from "Grandma." The lady shouted at JB, who responded by killing her with a handkerchief. These are the three murders for which she acknowledged responsibility, and for which she provided details during her initial interrogations.

According to JB's report, she used to observe her potential victims while they were shopping. She selected only old women who were alone. Initially, she approached them in a friendly way to win their confidence to such a point that the ladies would extend an invitation asking JB to come into their homes.

Between 2003 and 2006, a further nine elderly women were strangled in Mexico City within a relatively close geographical area. In some of the cases, burglary was thought to be the motive. Mexican policemen suspected that JB was the killer in all of these cases.

On interrogation by one of the examiners about the wrongness of killing people, JB recognized that she behaved inappropriately, because she knew the social rules, was aware of the basic meaning of the law, and also "knew that killing people is by all means unacceptable." But, on the other hand, JB stated that her actions were justified, because she felt victimized by the older women when they humiliated her on the basis of her social status. JB admitted to easily losing control and patience when she was judged and offended so unfairly.

Testing was carried out at the Reclusorio Santa Martha Acatitla (Mexico, D.F.). Two different types of tests were used: (1) neuropsychological and neuropsychiatric assessment and (2) electrophysiological studies.

The neuropsychological and neuropsychiatric assessment included NEUROPSI, a brief neuropsychological battery test for Spanish speakers (Ostrosky-Solís, Ardila, & Rosselli, 1999), and a frontal lobe battery test (Flores, Ostrosky, & Lozano, 2008). This battery of tests evaluates several executive functions related to different frontal systems. Depression and anxiety were assessed with the Beck Depression Inventory (Jurado et al., 1988) and the Beck Anxiety Inventory, respectively (Robles et al., 2001); both measures are validated for Mexican populations.

Psychopathy was assessed by using the Hare Psychotherapy Checklist-Revised (PCL-R) scale. Factor analytic studies have demonstrated that the scale has a two-factor structure: Factor 1 describes an affective and interpersonal style and Factor 2 describes an antisocial lifestyle.

The electrophysiological studies used electroencephalogram (EEG) analysis. The EEG was recorded for ten minutes with the eyes open and ten minutes with the eyes closed. A computerized system (Neuroscan 4.2, Charlotte, NC) recorded the EEG. Activity was recorded from electrodes placed in 32 different locations on the scalp according to the extended and standardized international 10–20 system. Event-related potentials (ERPs) were recorded while JB was viewing pictures of emotionally charged unpleasant scenes with and without moral content, as well as emotionally pleasant and neutral pictures. A total of 240 color pictures were used.

Table 5.3 presents the results of the different tests that were conducted. In NEUROPSI, JB's general cognitive functioning fitted into a normal range, given her age and education. Her verbal understanding was normal. She could correctly recognize passive and active sentences. Her attention and memory (verbal and non-verbal) corresponded to a normal range for her age and education. Her remote memory was well preserved; she could recall historical events and correctly describe her own life. The frontal lobe battery test scores were abnormally elevated, which is consistent with frontal brain dysfunction. For example, some motor difficulties were noted, such as when alternating movement between the hands, which was more evident in the right hand; she also experienced difficulties with the Opposite Reactions test. In the Beck Depression Inventory and the Beck Anxiety Inventory, she scored for slight depression and slight anxiety.

In the Hare PCL-R, JB obtained a score of 25 (out of a possible 40 points). Although she did not reach the cut-off point of 30 established for psychopaths,

TABLE 5.3 General results in the different neuropsychological and neuropsychiatric tests

Test	Score	Normative scores	Remarks
Neuropsychological tests			
NEUROPSI	80.5	68–94	Normal general cognitive function
Frontal lobe battery test	42.0	1–35	Defects in executive functioning: motor planning, alternate movement, and motor sequences
Neuropsychiatric tests			
Beck Depression Inventory	10	0–63	Slight depression
Beck Anxiety Inventory	9	0–63	Slight anxiety
Hare PCL-R	25	0–40	Psychopathic tendencies: higher scores on affective/interpersonal factor

some clear psychopathic tendencies may be assumed. JB displayed significantly higher scores on all the items that loaded on Factor 1 (affective interpersonal measures), and lower scores on Factor 2 (antisocial measures).

The EEG results revealed that her background activity consisted of well-developed, well-organized 8–9 Hz mid-voltage activity predominating posteriorly, with activation of the alpha rhythm with eye closure. The alpha rhythm was fairly well sustained during the course of the EEG. Occasional sharp focal activities were seen in the left fronto-central regions. This was matched less frequently by similar activity in the right hemisphere as well. However, such sharply contoured activity was far more frequent in the left hemisphere. Nonetheless, this slightly irritative activity in and of itself does not suggest the diagnosis of a seizure disorder. In addition, a diffuse slowing consisting of 1–4 Hz delta and 4–7 Hz theta activity was seen predominating over fronto-temporal and central areas of the left hemisphere. There were no significant additional asymmetries.

Average ERPs from a normal subject (same age and gender) and from JB are presented in Figure 5.1 for the four experimental conditions. In the normal subject, the emotional pictures (pleasant and unpleasant with and without moral content) evoked a larger late positive potential (LPP) between 400 and 650 milliseconds than neutral stimuli, mainly in centro-parietal areas of both hemispheres. The amplitude and the latency of this component were earlier for the unpleasant pictures without moral content. These results have been replicated in over 50 neurologically intact subjects.

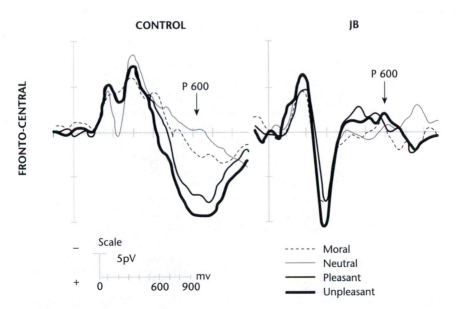

FIGURE 5.1 Average ERPs from a normal subject (same age and gender) and from JB for the four experimental conditions

Unlike the normal matched control, JB generated differences in the amplitude of the LPP between the neutral stimuli and the stimuli with emotional content. The LPP in response to the four types of stimuli was relatively small and brief, suggesting that JB processed all stimuli (neutral, pleasant, and unpleasant with and without moral content) differently from the normal participant. During the classification task, JB tended to score neutral stimuli as stimuli with emotional content. She also over-scored unpleasant stimuli. For instance, she scored a trash-can as pleasant with moral content because "it is used to keep order and cleanliness." JB only used extreme scores; that is, no intermediate values were recorded.

It was concluded that, in JB, genetic factors and/or environmental experience (e.g. childhood abuse) led to her having a psychopathic impairment in emotional processing (as revealed in the ERP data) and to the problematic behaviors identified through Factor 1 of the PCL-R (e.g. a lack of guilt and empathy, and pathological lying). A confluence of abuse during childhood, paranoid personality traits, some brain dysfunction, and a specific and unfavorable context resulted in a significant increase in JB's propensity for violent behavior.

References

Angrilli, A., Sartori, G., & Donzella, G. (2013). Cognitive, emotional and social markers of serial murdering. *The Clinical Neuropsychologist*, 27(3), 485–494.

Ardila, A., & Ostrosky-Solís, F. (2009). Neuropsicologia de los asesinos en serie [Neuropsychology of serial killers]. *Revista de Neurologia*, 48(3), 162–163.

Beasley, J.O. (2004). Serial murder in America: Case studies of seven offenders. *Behavioral Sciences & the Law*, 22(3), 395–414.

Boar, R., & Blundell, N. (1983). *The World's Most Infamous Murders*. London: Octopus.

Carlo, P. (2006). *The Ice Man: Confessions of a Mafia Contract Killer*. New York, NY: St. Martin's Press.

Douglas, J., Burgess, A.W., Burgess, A.G., & Ressler, R.K. (2013). *Crime Classification Manual: A Standard System for Investigating and Classifying Violent Crime*. San Francisco, CA: John Wiley & Sons.

Egger, S.A. (2002). *The Killers Among Us: An Examination of Serial Murder and Its Investigation*. Upper Saddle River, NJ: Prentice Hall.

Flores, J.C., Ostrosky, F., & Lozano, A. (2008). Bateria de funciones frontales y ejecutivas: presentacion [Neuropsychological battery for the evaluation of frontal lobe and executive functions]. *Neuropsicologia, Neuropsiquiatria y Neurociencias*, 8(1), 141–158.

Flowers, A. (1993). *Blind Fury*. New York, NY: Pinnacle Books.

Frei, A., Völlm, B., Graf, M., & Dittmann, V. (2006). Female serial killing: Review and case report. *Criminal Behaviour and Mental Health*, 16(3), 167–176.

Geary, R. (2003). *The Beast of Chicago: An Account of the Life and Crimes of Herman W. Mudgett, Known to the World as H. H. Holmes*. New York, NY: NBM Publishing.

Godwin, G.M. (2008). *Hunting Serial Predators*. Burlington, MA: Jones & Bartlett Learning.

Hare, R.D. (1999). *Without Conscience: The Disturbing World of the Psychopaths Among Us*. New York, NY: Guilford Press.

Hickey, E.W. (2012). *Serial Murderers and Their Victims*. Boston, MA: Cengage Learning.

Holmes, R., & Stephen, T. (1998). *Contemporary Perspectives on Serial Murder*. Thousand Oaks, CA: SAGE Publications.

Jurado, S., Villegas, M.E., Mendez, L., Rodriguez, F., Loperena, V., & Varela, R. (1988). La estandarizacion del inventario de depresion de Beck para los residentes de la ciudad de Mexico [Standardization of Beck Depression Inventory for a Mexican sample]. *Salud Mental*, 21(3), 26–31.

Kelleher, M.D., & Kelleher, C.L. (1998). *Murder Most Rare: The Female Serial Killer*. Westport, CT: Praeger.

Kelly, K., & Montane, D. (2011). *I Would Find a Girl Walking*. New York, NY: Berkley.

Kraemer, G.W., Lord, W.D., & Heilbrun, K. (2004). Comparing single and serial homicide offenses. *Behavioral Sciences & the Law*, 22(3), 325–343.

Krivich, M., & Olgin, O. (1993). *Comrade Chikatilo: The Psychopathology of Russia's Notorious Serial Killer*. Fort Lee, NJ: Barricade Books.

Linedecker, C.L. (1993). *The Man Who Killed Boys: The John Wayne Gacy, Jr. Story*. New York, NY: Macmillan.

Myers, W.C. (2004). Serial murder by children and adolescents. *Behavioral Sciences & the Law*, 22(3), 357–374.

Newton, M. (2000). *The Encyclopedia of Serial Killers*. New York, NY: Checkmark Books.

Norris, J. (1988). *Serial Killers: The Growing Menace*. New York, NY: Doubleday.

Ostrosky-Solís, F., Ardila, A., & Rosselli, M. (1999). NEUROPSI: A brief neuropsychological test battery in Spanish with norms by age and educational level. *Journal of the International Neuropsychological Society*, 5(5), 413–433.

Ostrosky-Solís, F., Vélez-García, A., Santana-Vargas, D., Pérez, M., & Ardila, A. (2008). A middle-aged female serial killer. *Journal of Forensic Sciences*, 53(5), 1223–1230.

Ressler, R.K. (1993). *Whoever Fights Monsters: My Twenty Years Tracking Serial Killers for the FBI*. New York, NY: Macmillan.

Ressler, R.K. (1998). *I Have Lived in the Monster: Inside the Minds of the World's Most Notorious Serial Killers*. New York, NY: Macmillan.

Reynolds, M. (2004). *Dead Ends: The Pursuit, Conviction and Execution of Female Serial Killer Aileen Wuornos, the Damsel of Death*. New York, NY: Macmillan.

Robles, R., Varela, R., Jurado, S., & Perez, F. (2001). Version mexicana del inventario de ansiedad de Beck: Propiedades psicometricas [Spanish version of Beck Depression Inventory]. *Revista Mexicana de Psicologia*, 18(2), 211–218.

Russell, S. (2002). *Lethal Intent: The Shocking True Story of One of America's Most Notorious Female Serial Killers*. New York, NY: Pinnacle.

Sanmartín, J. (2013). *La Violencia y Sus Claves* [*Violence and Its Clues*] (Vol. 9). Madrid, Spain: Editorial Ariel.

Segrave, K. (1992). *Women Serial and Mass Murderers: A Worldwide Reference, 1580 through 1990*. Jefferson, NC: McFarland & Company.

Skrapec, C.A. (2001). Phenomenology and serial murder asking different questions. *Homicide Studies*, 5(1), 46–63.

Thorne, T. (1997). *Countess Dracula*. London: Bloomsbury.

Thorwald, J., & Formosa, F. (1966). *El Siglo de la Investigación Criminal* [*The Century of Criminal Investigation*]. Barcelona, Spain: Editorial Labor.

Warren, J.I., Hazelwood, R.R., & Dietz, P.E. (1996). The sexually sadistic serial killer. *Journal of Forensic Sciences*, 41(6), 970–974.

Wilson, W., & Hilton, T. (1998). Modus operandi of female serial killers. *Psychological Reports*, 82(2), 495–498.

Wilson, C., & Seaman, D. (2007). *The Serial Killers: A Study in the Psychology of Violence*. London: Virgin Books.

Wuornos, A. (2006). *Monster: My True Story*. London: John Blake Publishing.

6

MASS MURDERERS

Introduction

Unlike a serial killer (who kills people one by one, over months or years), a mass murderer appears in an unexpected way, killing as many people as he or she can, and it is not unusual for him or her to finish his or her spree by committing suicide. None of this is strange in the United States, where mass murders have been committed since at least the mid-twentieth century. In 1949, Howard Unruh triggered a massacre that took, in addition to his own life, the lives of 13 people in Camden County, New Jersey (Douglas, Burgess, & Ressler, 1995). Fifty year later, two students, Eric Harris (18 years old) and Dylan Klebold (17 years old), would give the concept of mass murder a new dimension when, on April 20, 1999, they arrived at their school (Columbine High School) heavily armed, killing 13 people, wounding 24 others, and finishing the act with their suicides (Brown & Rob, 2002).

These massacres invariably arouse great debate in the United States. Psychologists, anthropologists, and sociologists try to get to the bottom of the problem by finding out what these murderers thought. Was the reason their lack of moral values? Were they bored? Was it because weapons can be bought in supermarkets? Did they experience childhood psychological trauma? Determining the reasons that make a person commit a mass murder is an extremely complicated task, mainly because these murderers carry inside themselves almost unique combinations of motives and psychological traumas that drive them to the violent act.

For American criminologists Ronald and Stephen Holmes (Holmes & Holmes, 2000, 2008), the mass murderer profile involves a significant family component (children of dysfunctional couples, child abuse, and drug and alcohol abuse), in conjunction with psychological alterations (suicidal tendencies, and poor frustration and anger management) and conditions (work abuse, discrimination) that generate an explosive charge of resentment and hate in situations that only the murderer can understand.

To try to solve this problem and establish a profile that could help American authorities to detect potential mass murderers among young people, the FBI's National Center for the Analysis of Violent Crime analyzed the life patterns and potential motives of mass murderers in 2000 and concluded that, from adolescence, some signs of homicidal behavior can be detected, such as violent resistance to school organization (O'Toole, 2000). However, this analysis also recognized that there are no rules that allow us to detect a murderer of this kind easily, and so it is not easy to prevent this kind of offense.

The Worst Civil Massacre in the United States

Some years ago, the worst civil massacre registered in the United States took place. We are talking about the case of the Korean student Cho Seung-Hui, who killed 32 students, left 38 wounded, and then committed suicide on April 17, 2007. This 23-year-old student of Virginia Polytechnic Institute grew up in a South Korean family that immigrated to the United States when Seung-Hui was 8 years old. One day, he decided to take his weapons into school and use them against his class-mates. How can we understand this phenomenon? How can we distinguish the young people who commit such murders?

Are Biological Factors at Work?

One of the most controversial topics is whether there are biological factors that determine the existence of homicidal behaviors on a large scale. A study conducted by Puerto Rican psychologist Angie Vázquez (n.d.) summarizes some of these factors, including:

- *Genetic disorders:* Alterations in the gene tryptophan hydroxylase (THP) can impede the processing of serotonin and obstruct the control of aggressive impulses (Antypa, Serretti, & Rujescu, 2013; Nielsen et al., 1994; Takahashi, Shiroishi, & Koide, 2014; Virkkunen et al., 1994).
- *Fetal disorders:* Fetal alcohol syndrome, which results from the mother ingesting large quantities of alcohol during pregnancy, seems to alter neurological systems that participate in the control of violent impulses (Kelly, Day, & Streissguth, 2000; Streissguth et al., 1991).
- *Physiological damage:* Impacts and traumas that cause damage to the frontal lobe of the brain seem to encourage the presence of violent behaviors by decreasing neurological activity in that area, minimizing self-control (Baguley, Cooper, & Felmingham, 2006; Kim, 2002). Frontal damage, which is observed very frequently in cases of cranial trauma, may significantly affect executive functions, including the ability to control emotions.

- *Hormonal disorders:* Excessive testosterone levels seem to induce potentially homicidal behaviors (Terburg, Morgan, & van Honk, 2009). In a classic study, Dabbs et al. (1995) studied 44,462 male subjects, finding a high incidence of and correlation among delinquency, drug abuse, a tendency towards excess, and risk-taking in those people who had higher than normal levels of testosterone. In prisons, they found that those convicts who had committed more violent crimes were the ones who had higher levels of testosterone.
- *Mental disorders:* The presence of illnesses such as schizophrenia and psychosis often leads to homicidal actions. In a recent study, Fazel et al. (2014) undertook a total population cohort study in Sweden of 24,297 patients with schizophrenia and related disorders between January 1972 and December 2009. Patients were matched by age and sex to people from the general population (n=485,940) and were also matched to unaffected sibling controls (n=26,357). First, the researchers investigated rates of conviction for violent offenses, of suicide, and of premature mortality. Second, they analyzed associations between these adverse outcomes and socio-demographic, individual, familial, and distal risk factors, for men and women separately. Finally, they assessed time trends in adverse outcomes between 1972 and 2009. They concluded that schizophrenia and related disorders are associated with substantially increased rates of violent crime, suicide, and premature mortality. Because of the size of the sample, the results can be considered quite reliable.

One Motive for Every Murderer

According to Ronald and Stephen Holmes (Holmes & Holmes, 2001, 2008), the motives of a mass murderer can be classified in the following six categories:

1. *Perverse love:* people who kill members of their family or their close affective environment suddenly to avenge unrequited love. *Example:* Ronald Gene Simmons murdered 14 family members after his wife threatened him with divorce. He was a 49-year-old retired United States Air Force master sergeant; in total, he killed 16 people over a week-long period in 1987. The first 14 victims were members of his family, including a daughter he had sexually abused and the child he had fathered with her.
2. *Politics:* murderers who are driven by ideological claims and decide to kill a group of people onto whom they project their hatred. *Example:* On February 25, 1994, a 37 year-old Israeli doctor and religious extremist named Baruch Goldstein went to the Cave of the Patriarchs (a sacred place for Jews, Muslims, and Christians) in the Palestine city of Hebron and shot freely, killing 29 Muslim Palestinians and wounding 150 more (Cohen & Susser, 2000).
3. *Revenge:* having suffered abuse, which can have lasted for several years, the person explodes in violent revenge against the abuser, such as a work boss, a

stalker, or a whole system that he or she considers to have been oppressing him or her. *Example:* On October 2, 2006, 32-year-old Charles Carl Roberts entered an Amish community school in Pennsylvania and killed five girls. Through contact with the murderer before he died, it was revealed that he wanted to avenge "something" that had happened to him 20 years previously (Kocieniewski, 2006).

4. *Sexual:* the control that the murderer exercises during the taking of hostages causes him or her sexual pleasure, which can be accompanied by rape before the killing. *Example:* On July 14, 1966, Richard Speck, who was 49 years old, murdered eight nurses in a Chicago hospital after raping them (Breo & Martin, 1993). David Cooke, Director of Forensic Psychology Services at the University of Glasgow, has thoroughly studied crimes with an entirely sexual motivation (Cooke, 2001). Cooke has proposed that there are differences between rapist-murderers who kill their victims to avoid being reported and consequently captured and those who are driven by a much deeper sadism, in which killing their victims is the aim, and who have no other considerations. According to Cooke, the first group of murderers do not gain sexual satisfaction by killing their victims, while the second group search for precisely that pleasure and this motivates them to commit the crime. In other words, the objective of this second group is to find an emotion strong enough to excite them and to give them as much satisfaction as possible. This group also often commit the sadist act of mutilating the victim, triggering fantasies in the psychopath.

5. *Execution:* a mass murder that is committed as collateral damage of a selective murder that is committed to settle scores. *Example:* On November 27, 1989, Pablo Escobar (39 years old at the time) ordered a bomb to be set off on Avianca Flight 203 between Bogota and Cali to kill the Colombian presidential candidate Cesar Gaviria, who cancelled his trip at the last minute. The Boeing 727-21 plane exploded and 110 people died (Bowden, 2009).

6. *Psychotic:* a mentally disturbed person butchers his or her victim during an episode of madness. *Example:* On April 28, 1996, a 28-year-old man named Martin Bryant, who had mental health problems and was apparently traumatized by his father's suicide, triggered a massacre in the Tasmanian city of Port Arthur, killing 35 people and wounding 24 more (Bingham, 1996).

Some Examples

Below are listed some of the most well-known mass murderers in the history of the United States:

*   *Timothy McVeigh*, 33 years old, and *Terry Nichols*, 40 years old (April 19, 1995). *Crime scene:* Alfred P. Murrah Federal Building, Oklahoma. *Method:* explosives. *Number killed:* 168 (Jones & Israel, 2001).

- *Julio González*, 36 years old (March 29, 1990). *Crime scene:* Happy Land social club, New York. *Method:* arson. *Number killed:* 87. *Note:* A quarrel with his girlfriend caused the attack (Barbanel, 1990).
- *Andrew Kehoe*, 55 years old (May 18, 1927). *Crime scene:* elementary school of Bath Township, Michigan. *Method:* explosives. *Number killed:* 45. *Note:* The motive of the attack was a tax that he considered opposed his interests (Parker, 1992).
- *David Burke*, 35 years old (December 7, 1987). *Crime scene:* Flight 1771 of Pacific Southwest Airlines. *Method:* shooting. *Number killed:* 43. *Note:* Burke killed his former boss, the pilot, the co-pilot, and a flight attendant in the plane, causing the plane to crash (Cummings, 1987).
- *George Hennard*, 35 years old (October 16, 1991). *Crime scene:* Luby's coffee shop, Killeen, Texas. *Method:* shooting. *Number killed:* 22. *Note:* Regarding the motive for the massacre, it is only known that the murderer shouted "This is what Bell County has done to me" before opening fire (Terry, 1991).
- *James Oliver Huberty*, 41 years old (July 18, 1984). *Crime scene:* McDonald's restaurant, San Ysidro, California. *Method:* shooting. *Number killed:* 21. *Note:* The murderer's widow tried to sue McDonald's, accusing it of including an additive in its hamburgers that caused her husband's madness (Cawthorne & Tibballs, 1994).
- *Charles Whitman*, 25 years old (July 31, 1966). *Crime scene:* university clock tower, Austin, Texas. *Method:* shooting. *Number killed:* 18. *Note:* It seems that a brain tumor caused the disturbance that led him to commit the murders (Lavergne, 1997).
- *James Holmes*, 25 years old (July 20, 2012). *Crime scene:* Century Movie Theater, Aurara, Colorado. *Method:* shooting using semi-automatic rifle and handgun, and tear gas grenades. *Number killed:* 12, and 70 injured. *Note:* He had previously consulted a psychiatrist; mental disorders are assumed (Ingold, 2012).

Why Do Mass Murderers Commit Their Crimes?

By analyzing specific cases of mass murderers, a series of questions emerge: Who are these individuals? What is their psychological profile? What drives them to kill generally unknown people? By comparing a variety of mass murderers, it can be seen that they seemingly show a series of common features that can help us to understand a little of their behavior:

- They are people with emotional disorders, and are in conflict, angry with the world, and depressed.
- They can be intelligent and capable, but they are not satisfied with their achievements; they often feel that they are treated unfairly by other people.

- Despite having some friends, they feel alone and isolated.
- They have hostile personalities, are very sensitive to criticism, and are resentful.
- They suffer from obsessive thoughts about injustices that they have suffered.
- They have fantasies of revenge and violence.
- For a high percentage of them, there is a triggering event in their lives, such as social rejection or disciplinary pressure from authority.
- As their depression increases, their judgment and perspective are distorted.
- They have suicidal personalities; they think that it is not worth living and that the only way to solve their problems is through death.

It is probably the simultaneous combination of a variety of factors that trigger killing sprees. José Sanmartín (Raine & Sanmartín, 2000; Sanmartín, 2013) suggests that there are several common characteristics in these murderers:

- They have a predisposition to violent behavior—in other words, a personality with psychopathic tendencies.
- There is evidence of emotional abuse. They feel rejected and start to shelter themselves in fantasies that allow them to overcome, at least in their imagination, their particular frustrations. Although we all fantasize, it is common for the fantasies of sadistic murderers, which they have often recreated in their imagination since adolescence, to have sexual components with significant violence.
- For a while, they shelter in fantasies to escape from frustrations, but possibly an event occurs that induces them to make these fantasies a reality. Fantasies are individual, but there are feelings of revenge in all of them. Anything can trigger the violence, even something that they have been experiencing for many years.

From the neurobiological point of view, it has been assumed that most organized murderers, who show predatory violence, probably have brain abnormalities such as a hyperactive amygdala and hypothalamus, brain areas that are related to certain emotional elements (LeDoux, 1998; Phelps & LeDoux, 2005). As previously mentioned, these are the brain regions that trigger fear and anger. Moreover, paralimbic system dysfunction has been related to an increase in violence (Anderson & Kiehl, 2014).

J. Reid Meloy and his team at the University of California in San Diego have used data from investigations conducted with reptiles and other animals to analyze the origin of these criminal behaviors (Meloy, 1992; Raine et al., 1998). The foundation on which these studies are based is that mammals, through the limbic system, have the ability to socialize in an emotional and sensitive way. By contrast, reptiles do not have a brain cortex and, therefore, lack the ability to emotionally respond to their offspring; reptiles also do not show another behavior exhibited in all mammals: forward-looking actions, such as the accumulation of food to cope with periods of shortage. Gathering food implies that mammals have the ability to plan for the future and anticipate unfavorable consequences. The psychopath, just like reptiles, either poorly anticipates future situations or is unable to anticipate unfavorable situations. In addition, the parental impulse of mammals, which is absent in most reptiles, reminds us of this lack of care towards offspring that is typical of psychopaths, as well as stories of abuse in many of their biographies. Finally, psychopaths share with reptiles the inability to socialize in an affective and genuinely expressive way, which explains their lack of empathy and significant bonds. Although this is merely an analogy, it suggests that psychopaths do not normally use certain anticipative and empathic abilities that clearly depend on the neocortex.

Environmental Pollution: Masters' Hypothesis

Some researchers have pointed out other possible causes in the development of a murderer who has a psychopathic personality. Roger Masters, a professor at Dartmouth College in New Hampshire, USA, has an interesting hypothesis, which supposes there is a relationship between pollution and violent crime in cities. Masters' study, in which he correlates pollution and crime in the context of environmental toxicology, remains a controversial article (Masters, Hone, & Doshi, 1998).

Masters makes a risky statement: that there is an association between environmental pollution and crime rates. In his study, he analyzed whether there was a correlation among socio-economic and demographic factors, poverty, population density, ethnic origin, unemployment, drug addiction, alcoholism, expulsion from school, and migration with criminal rates; however, he found no significant correlations or associations. By investigating other possible causes, he found a factor that linked the places with the least and the most criminality: the quantity of environmental pollution. He also found extensive scientific information about some kinds of pollutants that alter human physiology and affect some nervous control mechanisms, with which the behavior of individuals can be modified. He specifically studied lead and manganese, toxic metals that abound as residues of industrial processes and that affect nervous functions (Wright et al., 2008). High levels of lead cause damage to neuroglial cells, an important supporting tissue for brain neurons, while high levels of manganese decrease the release of serotonin and dopamine, two neurotransmitters associated with behavior impulses. According to Masters, when the human body absorbs these two pollutants, which are produced by foundries, chemical plants, leaded petrol, and piped water systems, among other sources, there is an adverse effect on the brain's ability to block violent responses.

He made his first investigations in convicts, and discovered that violent criminals had more lead and manganese in their bodies than non-violent criminals.

Other studies have revealed that children who have more significant behavioral problems have a larger quantity of lead in the blood (Stretesky & Lynch, 2001). Finally, Masters argues that environmental pollution rates could be as good as poverty in being a criminal indicator.

Although there are no definitive answers, his point of view continues to be controversial.

Psychological Factors: Walters' Model

As it is not possible to explain a mass murderer's behavior through physiology or genetics alone, it is also necessary to take into account environmental and psychological factors. If we use Glenn Walters' (1990) model as a basis, we can partially explain the psychological processes involved in criminal and violent behaviors, including mass murder.

Walters makes reference to the "criminal lifestyle," considering four factors: (1) conditions, (2) choice, (3) cognition, and (4) behavior. Criminals can act violently because they have a cognitive system that allows them to filter reality in a way that validates the desire to cause harm. Feelings such as self-exoneration allow the subject to disobey social rules, because, in this way, he or she eliminates all guilt or anxiety that would otherwise inhibit antisocial behavior. Other cognitive pairings such as permissiveness and power, sentimentalism and superoptimism, and cognitive indolence and inconsistency are linked to other behavior patterns: interpersonal intrusion, self-indulgence, and irresponsibility, respectively.

Through this model, it is possible to affirm that an individual will have a higher probability to kill, providing he or she has these different consolidated patterns of behavior that are enabled, at the same time, by a criminogenic thought. The origin of these behaviors and thoughts is where conditions and choice come into play. It should be noted that, by "conditions," Walters is referring to social, psychological, and physiological factors that predispose the subject to adopt a criminal lifestyle. In this way, individuals without attachment to prosocial models, with the urge for stimulation and poor self-esteem, find themselves in the right conditions to achieve an outcast status by using violence. These conditions, in Walters' opinion, generate a basic fear in relation to daily life tasks and responsibility, as they are faced with their incompetence in so many spheres of life.

The factors that induce an individual to kill, particularly to kill in large numbers and often to kill unknown people, are never easy to explain. To understand this phenomenon, an interdisciplinary approach between specialists from a variety of areas is important, including psychologists, sociologists, psychiatrists, neurologists, and biologists. Only in this way will it be possible to isolate social, geographic, biological, and economic variables to try to understand the enigmas of the criminal mind and to prevent other tragic cases such as those that humanity has already witnessed.

References

Anderson, N.E., & Kiehl, K.A. (2014). Psychopathy: Developmental perspectives and their implications for treatment. *Restorative Neurology and Neuroscience*, 32(1), 103–117.

Antypa, N., Serretti, A., & Rujescu, D. (2013). Serotonergic genes and suicide: A systematic review. *European Neuropsychopharmacology*, 23(10), 1125–1142.

Baguley, I.J., Cooper, J., & Felmingham, K. (2006). Aggressive behavior following traumatic brain injury: How common is common? *The Journal of Head Trauma Rehabilitation*, 21(1), 45–56.

Barbanel, J. (1990). Fire in the Bronx; tracing the club's owners. *New York Times*, March 27.

Bingham, M. (1996). *Suddenly One Sunday*. New York, NY: HarperCollins.

Bowden, M. (2009). *Killing Pablo*. London: Atlantic Books.

Breo, D.L., & Martin, W.J. (1993). *The Crime of the Century: Richard Speck and the Murder of Eight Student Nurses*. New York, NY: Bantam Books.

Brown, B., & Rob, M. (2002). *No Easy Answers: The Truth Behind Death at Columbine*. New York, NY: Lantern Books.

Cawthorne, N., & Tibballs, G. (1994). *Killers: Contract Killers, Spree Killers, Sex Killers— The Ruthless Exponents of Murder, the Most Evil Crime of All*. London: Boxtree.

Cohen, A., & Susser, B. (2000). *Israel and the Politics of Jewish Identity: The Secular–Religious Impasse*. Baltimore, MD: Johns Hopkins University Press.

Cooke, D. (2001). Psychopathy, sadism and serial killing. In: Raine, A., & Sanmartín, J. (eds), *Violence and Psychopathy*. New York, NY: Springer.

Cummings, J. (1987). Kin of suspect defiant and contrite. *New York Times*, December 11.

Dabbs Jr, J.M., Carr, T.S., Frady, R.L., & Riad, J.K. (1995). Testosterone, crime, and misbehavior among 692 male prison inmates. *Personality and Individual Differences*, 18(5), 627–633.

Douglas, J.E., Burgess, A.W., & Ressler, R.K. (1995). *Sexual Homicide: Patterns and Motives*. New York, NY: The Free Press.

Fazel, S., Wolf, A., Palm, C., & Lichtenstein, P. (2014). Violent crime, suicide, and premature mortality in patients with schizophrenia and related disorders: A 38-year total population study in Sweden. *The Lancet Psychiatry*, 1(1), 44–54.

Holmes, R., & Holmes, S. (2000). *Murder in America*. Thousand Oaks, CA: SAGE Publications.

Holmes, R., & Holmes, S. (2001). *Mass Murder in the United States*. Upper Saddle River, NJ: Prentice Hall.

Holmes, R., & Holmes, S. (2008). *Profiling Violent Crimes: An Investigative Tool*. Thousand Oaks, CA: SAGE Publications.

Ingold, J. (2012). James Holmes faces 142 counts, including 24 of first-degree murder. *The Denver Post*, July 30.

Jones, S., & Israel, P. (2001). *Others Unknown: Timothy McVeigh and the Oklahoma City Bombing Conspiracy* (2nd edn). New York, NY: PublicAffairs.

Kelly, S.J., Day, N., & Streissguth, A.P. (2000). Effects of prenatal alcohol exposure on social behavior in humans and other species. *Neurotoxicology and Teratology*, 22(2), 143–149.

Kim, E. (2002). Agitation, aggression, and disinhibition syndromes after traumatic brain injury. *NeuroRehabilitation*, 17(4), 297–310.

Kocieniewski, D. (2006). Man shoots 11, killing 5 girls, in Amish school. *New York Times*, October 3.

Lavergne, G.M. (1997). *A Sniper in the Tower: The Charles Whitman Murders*. Denton, TX: University of North Texas Press.

LeDoux, J. (1998). *The Emotional Brain: The Mysterious Underpinnings of Emotional Life.* New York, NY: Simon & Schuster.

Masters, R.D., Hone, B.T., & Doshi, A. (1998). Environmental pollution, neurotoxicity, and criminal violence. In: Rose, J. (ed.), *Environmental Toxicology.* New York, NY: Gordon & Breach Science Publishers. pp. 13–48.

Meloy, J.R. (1992). *The Psychopathic Mind: Origins, Dynamics, and Treatment.* Lanham, MD: Rowman & Littlefield.

Nielsen, D.A., Goldman, D., Virkkunen, M., Tokola, R., Rawlings, R., & Linnoila, M. (1994). Suicidality and 5-hydroxyindoleacetic acid concentration associated with a tryptophan hydroxylase polymorphism. *Archives of General Psychiatry,* 51(1), 34–38.

O'Toole, M.E. (2000). *The School Shooter: A Threat Assessment Perspective.* New York, NY: National Center for the Analysis of Violent Crime.

Parker, G. (1992). *Mayday: History of a Village Holocaust.* Battle Creek, MI: Michigan Liberty Press.

Phelps, E.A., & LeDoux, J.E. (2005). Contributions of the amygdala to emotion processing: From animal models to human behavior. *Neuron,* 48(2), 175–187.

Raine, A., & Sanmartín, J. (eds). (2000). *Violencia y Psicopatía* [*Violence and Psychopathy*] (Vol. 4). Madrid, Spain: Editorial Ariel.

Raine, A., Meloy, J.R., Bihrle, S., Stoddard, J., LaCasse, L., & Buchsbaum, M.S. (1998). Reduced prefrontal and increased subcortical brain functioning assessed using positron emission tomography in predatory and affective murderers. *Behavioral Sciences & the Law,* 16(3), 319–332.

Sanmartín, J. (2013). *La Violencia y Sus Claves* [*Violence and Its Clues*] (Vol. 9). Madrid, Spain: Editorial Ariel.

Streissguth, A.P., Aase, J.M., Clarren, S.K., Randels, S.P., LaDue, R.A., & Smith, D.F. (1991). Fetal alcohol syndrome in adolescents and adults. *JAMA,* 265(15), 1961–1967.

Stretesky, P.B., & Lynch, M.J. (2001). The relationship between lead exposure and homicide. *Archives of Pediatrics & Adolescent Medicine,* 155(5), 579–582.

Takahashi, A., Shiroishi, T., & Koide, T. (2014). Genetic mapping of escalated aggression in wild-derived mouse strain MSM/Ms: Association with serotonin-related genes. *Frontiers in Neurosciences,* 8: 156.

Terburg, D., Morgan, B., & van Honk, J. (2009). The testosterone–cortisol ratio: A hormonal marker for proneness to social aggression. *International Journal of Law and Psychiatry,* 32(4), 216–223.

Terry, D. (1991). Portrait of Texas killer: Impatient and troubled. *New York Times,* October 18.

Vazquez, A. (n.d.). Psicología forense: Sobre las causas de la conducta criminal [Forensic psychology: On the causes of criminal behavior]. *Robertexto.* Retrieved on December 13, 2014 from: www.robertexto.com/archivo13/psicol_forense.htm.

Virkkunen, M., Rawlings, R., Tokola, R., Poland, R.E., Guidotti, A., Nemeroff, C., ... & Linnoila, M. (1994). CSF biochemistries, glucose metabolism, and diurnal activity rhythms in alcoholic, violent offenders, fire setters, and healthy volunteers. *Archives of General Psychiatry,* 51(1), 20–27.

Walters, G. (1990). *The Criminal Lifestyle.* Newbury Park, NY: SAGE Publications.

Wright, J.P., Dietrich, K.N., Ris, M.D., Hornung, R.W., Wessel, S.D., Lanphear, B.P., & Rae, M.N. (2008). Association of prenatal and childhood blood lead concentrations with criminal arrests in early adulthood. *PLoS Medicine,* 5(5), e101.

7

CANNIBALISM

Introduction

Few human behaviors induce such contradictory feelings of horror and fascination as cannibalism. Whether in the stories of the survivors of the 1972 Andes plane crash (Read, 2005) or in Thomas Harris' series of novels about Hannibal Lecter (Harris, 1981, 1988, 2006), the consumption of human flesh is an extreme behavior that produces an intense emotional response that is often associated with abnormal circumstances or primitive civilizations.

Cannibalism (or "anthropophagy" in the case of human beings, from the Greek *anthropos*, meaning "man," and *phagia*, meaning "action of eating") can be defined as the act of eating members of one's own species. However, this extreme behavior is not seen in the human being exclusively; it also occurs in animals such as the black widow spider (which devours its partner after copulation), some types of sharks (where one fetus eats others in the uterus of the mother) and mammals such as the leopard and even the chimpanzee (Polis, 1981). However, studies conducted at Vanderbilt University found that these practices are often the result of sex drives or poor feeding conditions, the latter generally when larger animals eat puppies or weaker animals (Salisbury, 2001). But, unlike animals, human beings have also been known to eat members of their own species for religious or symbolic reasons. In Greek mythology, an act of cannibalism happens in Olympus, where the god Saturn devours his children so that they do not steal his powers. However, it was not until the sixteenth century, when European explorers conducted voyages of discovery and the printing press was invented, that the modern concept of a "cannibal" was created (Salisbury, 2001).

The origin of the word "cannibal" is interesting; it comes from Spanish. During one of his voyages of exploration, Christopher Columbus encountered a tribe called "Caribbean," whose members participated in rituals that involved ingesting fresh human flesh. Explorers mispronounced the name of the tribe and called them "Canibs," a word that eventually became "cannibals." In the same way, people such as the Fore from Papua New Guinea, the Aghoris from India, the Chilean Mapuche, the Paraguayan Guaraní, and even the Mexican Aztecs were identified as cannibals based initially on true events (a famine in 1554 triggered acts of cannibalism among the Mapuche, for example) but also motivated by the desire to nourish the nascent industry of books on discovered lands, with such books illustrated with scenes of cannibal feasts (Diehl & Donnelly, 2012; Vramescu, 2009).

During the nineteenth century, a kind of narrative appeared about cannibalism that made reference not to exotic people, but to cases of explorers who have to eat human flesh to survive. Famous cases include the *Medusa*, a French ship that ran aground on the African coast in 1816, whose castaways had to devour corpses; the group of 33 settlers called the "Donner Party" who were trapped by snow on the border between California and Nevada, and who in the winter of 1847 ate half a dozen corpses; and the most famous example in our history: Uruguayan Air Force Flight 571, which crashed in the South American Andes in 1972, with the survivors having to eat the bodies of their comrades to be able to survive (Read, 2005).

However, in the twentieth century, cannibalism was related not only to acts of desperation, but also to political decisions: between 1932 and 1933, there was an extreme shortage of food in Ukraine, triggering a famine during which many instances of cannibalism were recorded. Similarly, during the final stages of the siege of Leningrad (between 1941 and 1944) in World War II, cases of cannibalism occurred due to the food shortage caused by the blockade of supplies. In the middle of the twentieth century, among guerrillas such as the Leopard Society in the African nation of Liberia and the MauMau in Kenya, there were recorded cases of cannibalism of prisoners.

It was also in the twentieth century that criminal cannibals appeared, including the American Albert Fish, who in 1928 killed and ate parts of a girl named Grace Budd (Kray, 2007), and Andrei Chikatilo, who killed 50 people and ate their body parts in the former Soviet Union in the 1970s and 1980s (Krivich & Olgin, 1993). But perhaps the most famous homicidal cannibal in recent times is Jeffrey Dahmer, who murdered and ate the bodies of some of his 17 victims, becoming a "celebrity" in the mass media (Davis, 1991).

However, in spite of its importance, the case of Jeffrey Dahmer was not the first case of cannibalism in which the culprit would become famous. In June 1981, the Japanese criminal Issei Sagawa murdered a Dutch student of literature, Renée Hartevelt, in Paris and, over several days, removed the flesh from her buttocks to cook it or eat it raw. He was captured after trying to get rid of the human remains, but, due to a series of legal technicalities, he was released in Japan in 1986, where he has lived freely since, writing articles and even starring in horror films as an actor (Morris, 2007).

Types of Cannibalism

Disregarding cannibalism that results from famine, criminal acts of cannibalism can be classified in several ways. In anthropology, several attempts have been made to distinguish between different types of cannibalism (e.g. Bahn, 1991), and it could be considered that there are at least the following subgroups: (1) sexual, (2) aggressive, (3) spiritual and ritual, (4) nutritional, and (5) epicurean (devoted to pleasure). However, this classification is not strict and it is possible that a particular case can fall into several of these categories.

Sexual cannibalism is considered a form of sexual sadism and is often associated with necrophilia (sex with corpses). Cases that have involved sexual cannibalism include Andrei Chikatilo, who could only achieve sexual arousal during the murder and ingestion of his victims (Krivich & Olgin, 1993). A book written by Clara Bruce entitled *Chew On This: You're What's for Dinner* (1999) points out that some cannibals say that they achieve orgasm by eating flesh, while others report extracorporeal experiences and compare its effect with drugs such as mescaline. A study conducted at Eastern University, Illinois, in 2002 analyzed groups of students who were asked about cannibalism and sexual interests. The study revealed that, if they had to eat a person, most people would rather eat a person to whom they were sexually attracted. This suggests that there may be a sexual component to the practice of cannibalism.

Aggressive cannibalism may be motivated by a desire to express control or power over the victim. It is the ultimate expression of domination over the other person and may be motivated by feelings of hostility or fear, creating the need to exert power and revenge through murder and then eating the corpse. One example is the case of Anna Zimmerman, a 26-year-old German woman and mother of two children who, in 1981, killed her boyfriend in a fit of rage; she dismembered his body, froze the parts, and was gradually cooking portions, serving them to her children for dinner (Berry-Dee, 2011). A similar case was that of Trinidad Ramirez, a woman from Mexico City who murdered her partner in 1971; she dismembered the body, removing pieces of flesh to use them as a filling for tamales. However, in this case (known as "la Tamalera") she always said that she did it for practical reasons—that is, to save some money.

The main characteristic of *spiritual and ritual cannibalism* is the desire to obtain the virtues or spiritual characteristics of the victim. Jeffrey Dahmer reported that, when he consumed his victims, he believed that spiritually the victims became part of him (Davis, 1991). Such cannibals also believe that their cannibalism allows them to absorb some of the victim's attributes, such as in the case of Armin Meiwes, who declared in prison that he had absorbed the ability to speak English from his victim (Jewkes & Yar, 2013).

Nutritional cannibalism is the consumption of human flesh motivated mainly by the flavor of the flesh or its nutritional values. This type of cannibalism is rare and is considered a derivation of other forms, such as survival and sexual cannibalism.

Although it is not common, there are cases that fall into this category. In France, Nicolas Claux was sentenced in 1994 for the murder of 34-year-old Thierry Bissonier; he admitted that, while working in the Paris Saint Joseph Hospital, he took advantage of his position as an assistant and took flesh from the corpses deposited there to eat raw at his home.

Finally, *epicurean or pleasure cannibalism* overlaps with some of the previous forms, such as sexual and nutritional cannibalism.

The Case of Armin Meiwes

An exemplary case of the complexities of cannibalism occurred in 2001 when Armin Meiwes, a computer technician in the German city of Rothenburg, contacted 43-year-old Bernd-Juergen Brandes over the internet, with the explicit purpose of eating him. On March 21, they met at Meiwes' home and, in a room that was prepared with a cot, a cage, chains, and cooking implements, they succumbed to an act of cannibalism recorded entirely on video, being perhaps the first of its kind (Jewkes & Yar, 2013).

First, Brandes swallowed 20 sleeping pills and half a bottle of cherry schnapps liqueur. Meiwes then tried unsuccessfully to bite off his penis; he was only able to bite off his testicles. He then took a knife and cut off the penis of his partner. First, they tried to eat it raw, but, because it was too hard, they had to fry it with oil and garlic. However, the penis was burned in the process. Meiwes took his victim to the bathroom, where he was bleeding for some hours before Meiwes cut his throat in one blow, but not without first sealing the murder with a kiss. However, the feast did not finish there. Brandes' body was dismembered and the flesh was removed from the bones. The pieces of flesh (about 20 kilos) were kept in the freezer and were consumed over the following months, until, in December 2001, he was captured by the German authorities after he tried to contact more men on forums dedicated to homicidal fantasy.

The criminal case against Meiwes was conducted without major complications. Meiwes described his motive: "My idea was that he became part of my body." Later he added: "But I remembered [Brandes] on each piece of flesh that I ate. It was like receiving communion"; he even said that "the time of death was terrible; I felt hatred, anger, and happiness at the same time. I had wished for this all my life."

But these statements were not the only thing that attracted attention; Meiwes' explanations about his past showed him to be a man whose cannibalistic desires had been developing over his whole life. His interest in cannibalism emerged when he was between 8 and 12 years old, when he fantasized about eating his classmates at school. He recalled that, at that time, he lived alone with his mother and felt abandoned; he was obsessed with the idea of having a little brother: "someone who was part of me." So he created an imaginary brother, whom he called Frank. In addition, Meiwes said that the idea of cutting a human body aroused him sexually and to stimulate his fantasies he watched zombie and murder movies.

Now, Meiwes is serving a life sentence, but this has not been without legal dispute because cannibalism is not a crime in Germany. In addition, the victim explicitly asked to be ingested. The first sentence against him, issued in 2004, of eight years in prison for murder and disturbance of the peace of the dead had to be revised one year later and, in 2006, he was sentenced to life imprisonment.

However, the assessment of this case also involves an assessment of Bernd-Juergen Brandes, a man who, despite having a stable life and a girlfriend, maintained a parallel homosexual life in which he asked his lovers to hit and assault him with sharp items. Brandes' behavior can therefore surely be considered within the concept of suicide. The means that he employed to commit suicide was another man. His idea of transcendence was incorporating himself into the body of another person. Speculating, we could say that Brandes allowed Meiwes to take charge of his life by eating his body. Brandes, from a certain point of view, was not a victim because he was in control of his fate. He left his documents in order, bought a one-way ticket to Rothenburg, and freely met with his instrument of death. He insisted on certain conditions in the rite of his death. He forced Meiwes to cut off his penis and later saw his penis in Meiwes' mouth as a bizarre sexual act. He demanded that Meiwes cause him pain by cutting his body. The slow bleeding lasted for ten hours—enough time, at least in the early hours, to turn back, to stop, to avoid death. He did not do it. His determination was unwavering.

Cannibalism in Mexico

Mexico has a history of cannibalism. Pre-Hispanic documents such as the Codex Magliabechiano and the Florentino Codex (Aztec codices are books written by pre-Columbian and Colonial Aztecs of that period) and the chronicles of Bernal Díaz del Castillo (Díaz del Castillo, 1844) point out that, after the Aztec sacrifice of prisoners, the corpses (with the hearts extracted to satisfy the Gods) were thrown from the top of the ceremonial pyramids to dismember them, and were then cooked in stews by the public. It has never been clear whether this act of cannibalism was symbolic, motivated by religious issues, or a way to compensate for low protein in the Nahuatl diet.

This practice was stopped by the conquerors; cannibalism was for centuries something that only appeared as part of the methods that the Inquisition applied against heretics and sorcerers. Although there were food shortages in Mexico (especially after the wars and military uprisings that characterized the nineteenth century and part of the twentieth century), cases of cannibalism were not recorded until 1971, when the aforementioned Trinidad Ramirez was sentenced for killing and decapitating her husband and using his flesh to fill tamales.

It was not until two decades later that new cases of cannibalism in Mexico appeared. As detailed by Ricardo Ham in his book *México y Sus Asesinos Seriales*

(*Mexico and Its Serial Killers*; Ham, 2007), in 1998 in the city of Chihuahua, a man named Gilberto Ortega worked as a police officer in the village Doctor Belisario Dominguez and as a volunteer in the campaign of a candidate for federal congress. Ortega was accused and convicted of the murder of an 11-year-old boy and one of his neighbors, but it was not until 2003 that he confessed to having killed four of his relatives (who abused him when he was a child) and another 20 people; he confessed to having extracted the intestines of several of them to eat them cooked. However, he argued that the person responsible for the murders was an imaginary friend named Joel.

The year 2004 could be considered the year of cannibal actions in Mexico. On January 14, in the town of Las Galeras in Indaparapeo, Michoacan, a man named Francisco Maldonado killed his father, a farmer named Felix Maldonado, using a machete to open his skull. Although early studies into this case only mentioned homicide (and the fact that the father had abused his son, who was 44 years old at the time, all of his life), later statements found that the son had not only cut open his father's skull, but had devoured the brain, while experiencing hallucinations of a family fight. In addition, in December of that year, the beaches of the Mexican Caribbean witnessed one of the most extreme acts of cannibalism ever performed in the country. On December 14, 2004, the police arrested—in an abandoned palapa at the edge of Playa del Carmen—Gumaro de Dios Arias, a 26-year-old construction worker, who was addicted to drugs and had killed and cooked various parts of another man, presumably a soldier, known only by the nickname "Gaucho." Apparently, Gumaro had killed his partner during a discussion about drugs and sex on December 12. He then hung the corpse to be bled and smashed the head with a brick; later he took out the entrails, some of the ribs, the heart, and steaks from a leg. After having prepared a special sauce, the murderer ate the leg steaks. He decided on something different for the heart and ribs: he put them on a grill to be roasted on a low heat. The entrails he put in a saucepan to cook as a broth; he ate a kidney from this broth. His crime would have gone unnoticed if an acquaintance, who was passing by, had not seen the macabre scene. Since his arrest, he has been detained in prisons in Quintana Roo and Morelos; he is now waiting for the end of his life, as he contracted AIDS. In addition, according to psychologists who have analyzed him, he is suffering from severe schizophrenia.

The Case of José Luis Calva Zepeda

The mother of Alejandra Galeana Garavito, José Luis Calva Zepeda's last victim, said that, although she did not sympathize with him when she met him: "He behaved normally. He tried to be funny; he joked, tried to please us, and wanted to fit into the family." José Luis Zepeda Kawa, Luis Pavón, or, his real name, José Luis Calva Zepeda, was a seemingly nice, cultured man and resident of Building 198, Mosqueta Street, Guerrero, Mexico City.

The initial report of the General Attorney of Mexico City (PGJDF) notes that: "On Monday, October 8, 2007, in the early morning on the streets of Guerrero and Mosqueta, Guerrero, judicial police captured a person said to be named José Luis Calva Zepeda, after an accusation made by Soledad Garavito Fernández about the disappearance of her 32-year-old daughter named Alejandra Galeana Garavito." A few lines later, the report takes an unexpected turn: "Calva Zepeda affirmed that he had not seen her [the missing person] over the previous 15 days. After a request by the police, he allowed them to enter his apartment, which was dark. He took advantage of this circumstance and ran to the door of the balcony overlooking the street, where he tried to escape. However, the subject lost his balance and fell to the street, where he was eventually captured, having sustained a traumatic brain injury, a cervical sprain, and some abrasions to the skin as a result of the fall." In the morning, the agents made an inventory: "checking inside the apartment, the body of Alejandra Galeana Garavito was found in the closet of the bedroom. The body was dismembered: the right arm from the elbow and the right leg from the knee were missing; these body parts were found in the refrigerator." The report also notes that "two knives, a razor, and a pair of shoelaces with blood spots on them were found. On the stove, a pan containing leftovers of fat and fried flesh was found. Under the sink, a cereal box was found, inside which were bone remains covered with muscle tissue, which had been fried. A plate with cutlery and scraps of fried flesh was also found on the table." They also found copies of two novels, *Caminando Ando* and *La Noche Anterior*, in which the image of the probable guilty person appears along with a biographical sketch, in which he calls himself a journalist, poet, novelist and playwright, who has written more than 800 poems, ten novels and eight plays and among his most significant works are *Réquiem para un Alma en Pena* (a satirical drama), *Krish el Aprendiz de Mago* (a children's novel), *Antigua* (a fantasy novel), *Prostituyendo mi Alma* (poetry), and the eloquent *Instintos Caníbales* (a thriller). The following closes the report: "The cause of death of Alejandra Galeana Garavito was asphyxia because of armed strangulation and traumatic brain injury."

By the end of October 2007, Calva Zepeda had recovered from his injuries at Xoco Hospital, but reporters and judicial inquiries had begun to reveal parts of his early life: at an early age, his father died; his mother kept him in a state of semi-abandonment and he was sexually abused when he was 7 years old. In addition, he was convicted at least three times of robbery and sexual abuse and he had a relationship with a man named Juan Pablo Monroy. He supported himself by selling his literature door to door and, although he did not study at university, he portrayed himself to women as an intellectual and a journalist. A former partner of the alleged murderer revealed his abuse, his addiction to drugs and alcohol, and his fondness for black magic and movies showing zoophilia, sadomasochism, and serial killers. In addition, the murders of two other people were imputed to him: Verónica Consuelo Martínez Casarrubia, a drugstore assistant whose body was found in a cemetery of the Chimalhuacán municipality in 2004, and an anonymous prostitute whose dismembered body was found in the Tlatelolco housing complex in April 2007.

By the end of October, Calva Zepeda's file had been consigned to a judge in the Northern Prison; he admitted that he had killed and dismembered his partner, but said that he had cooked her to feed her to the dogs; he said he killed Alejandra because she had refused to give him a son and she began to show indifference towards him. Justice progressed at an unusual speed in the legal world and, on November 1, the judge sent him to prison for charges of aggravated murder and the desecration of a corpse. However, Calva Zepeda was not shaken by this; he began planning a novel that would, apparently, launch him into literary stardom, something for which he had long yearned. However, his novel, *Caníbal: Un Poeta Seductor*, remained unfinished when on the morning of December 11, 2007, he was found dead in his cell at the Eastern Penitentiary, hanged with a belt.

Calva Zepeda had the characteristic profile of a psychopath, with possible psychotic breaks. His abuse of drugs such as cocaine could have caused auditory or visual hallucinations. In addition, although psychopaths are individuals with severe personality disorders, they do not have serious alterations in their perception and superficial thought (Patrick, 2005). Psychopaths are people who often display great superficial charm, which, in conjunction with moral flexibility and a lack of remorse, allows them to be functional and successful members of society and at the same time to seduce their victims and attract them to their place of execution.

Calva Zepeda's acts of devouring his girlfriend and dismembering two other victims were not acts of sudden inspiration, but the product of a fantasy related to rage, masochism, a sadistic personality, sexuality linked to death, and probably the abuse that he suffered during his childhood. Undoubtedly, all these experiences molded and shaped his brain; such wicked thoughts are usually fed by pornography, in this case movies showing zoophilia and the literature of the Marquis de Sade; driven by other factors such as drug use or dissatisfaction, those thoughts led his actions to the extreme.

The act of eating the corpse could have symbolic implications, suggesting that the murderer believes that "you cannot live outside me and I cannot mix emotionally with you. Therefore, I have contact with you through the stomach and not through my feelings." When Calva Zepeda decided to kill, it is very probable that his ultimate objective was to humiliate his victim and, in this way, to experience power, recover his authority, and strengthen his self-esteem. Thus, the main motive of this murderer was probably a desire for domination and superiority.

Calva Zepeda's family buried his corpse on December 12, 2007, in the Cemetery of San Lorenzo Tezonco. A floral arrangement that was set on his grave read "Seductive Poet. Your siblings will never forget you."

References

Bahn, P. (1991). Is cannibalism too much to swallow? *New Scientist*, 130(1766), 38–40.

Berry-Dee, C. (2011). *Cannibal Serial Killers: Profiles of Depraved Flesh-Eating Murderers.* Berkeley, CA: Ulysses Press.

Bruce, C. (1999). *Chew On This: You're What's for Dinner*. New York, NY: Crave.

Davis, D. (1991). *The Jeffrey Dahmer Story: An American Nightmare*. London: Macmillan.

Díaz del Castillo, B. (1844). *The Memoirs of the Conquistador Bernal Díaz del Castillo* (translated by John Ingram Lockhart). London: J. Hatchard & Son.

Diehl, D., & Donnelly, M.F. (2012). *Eat Thy Neighbour: A History of Cannibalism*. London: The History Press.

Ham, R. (2007). *México y Sus Asesinos Seriales* [*Mexico and Its Serial Killers*]. Mexico D.F.: SamSara.

Harris, R. (1981). *Red Dragon*. New York, NY: Penguin Putnam.

Harris, R. (1988). *The Silence of the Lambs*. New York, NY: St. Martin's Press.

Harris, T. (2006). *Hannibal Rising*. New York, NY: Delacorte Press.

Jewkes, Y., & Yar, M. (2013). *Handbook of Internet Crime*. London: Routledge.

Kray, K. (2007). *The World's 20 Worst Crimes: True Stories of 20 Killers and Their 1000 Victims*. London: John Blake Publishing.

Krivich, M., & Olgin, O. (1993). *Comrade Chikatilo: The Psychopathology of Russia's Notorious Serial Killer*. Fort Lee, NJ: Barricade Books.

Morris, S. (2007). Issei Sagawa: Celebrity cannibal. *New Criminologist, the Online Journal of Criminology*, 32(5). Retrieved on January 5, 2017 from: https://web.archive.org/web/20110714172725/http://www.newcriminologist.com/article.asp?nid=17.

Patrick, C. (2005). *Handbook of Psychopathy*. New York, NY: Guilford Press.

Polis, G.A. (1981). The evolution and dynamics of intraspecific predation. *Annual Review of Ecology and Systematics*, 12(1), 225–251.

Read, P.P. (2005). *Alive: Sixteen Men, Seventy-Two Days, and Insurmountable Odds—The Classic Adventure of Survival in the Andes*. New York, NY: HarperCollins.

Salisbury, D.F. (2001). Brief history of cannibal controversies. *Exploration: The Online Research Journal of Vanderbuilt University*, August 15. Retrieved on August 22, 2017 from: http://exploration.vanderbilt.edu/news/news_cannibalism_pt2.htm#to.

Vramescu, C. (2009). *An Intellectual History of Cannibalism*. Princeton, NJ: Princeton University Press.

8

MEXICAN HITMEN

Introduction

The total number of deaths is terrifying: by 2015, more than 100,000 people had been killed since the so-called "Drug War" began in March 2006, its ignition being one of the first actions of Felipe Calderón Hinojosa's government. Like never before, sensationalist journalists needed to broaden their range of adjectives to describe the "Dantesque" and "diabolical" scenes that Mexican society began to witness from that moment.

The settling of scores, a power struggle, and savage rivalry caused the sudden demand for a dark and old trade: hitmen or hired killers. However, unlike the hitmen of the past (the Spanish word *sicario* comes from the Latin *sicarii*, the plural of *sicarium*, meaning someone who uses a dagger, a contract killer, or a killer on demand), Mexican hitmen were now armed with AK-47s, came from over the unguarded American border, and were trained not only to carry out the murders for which they were hired, but also to commit them with amazing and intimidating brutality for the benefit of both their rivals and the rest of society.

Who are these fearsome human resources? Hitmen are mostly young males between 19 and 25 years old, who are unlikely to pass the age of 30 because they will likely die as victims of the violence to which they contribute. Hitmen are considered by the leaders of criminal associations as disposable elements. The average working life of someone who joins a drug-trafficking organization as a hitman is no more than three years.

Nowadays, hitmen, unlike those Romans who killed under strict rules of discretion, have a characteristic modus operandi, and their way of carrying out a "job" differs significantly from that of other kinds of killers. Through various studies carried out in some federal prisons, it has been possible to determine a stereotypical profile for different kinds of killers (Ostrosky et al., 2011). In this way, it is possible to identify the following kinds of hitmen:

- *Public:* eliminates the "target" without worrying about the presence of other people. The killer makes it seem like a theft or an act of terrorism (also eliminating the people who are close to the target), or simply surprises the target head-on.
- *Clean:* only eliminates the target when there are no witnesses (if there were witnesses, they would also be eliminated) in a fast and blunt way.
- *Disguised:* eliminates the target by feigning a situation that could pass as an accident, suicide, or any other event that is far from the reality.

In general, hitmen work for all kinds of people and are hired both by low-income people and in organized crime. Consequently, the quantity of money that they receive for their "services" also varies depending on the fame that they have obtained, their skill, and the person who will be their victim. For example, if the target is an ordinary person, the payment will be lower than if the target is an influential or well-known person, such as a businessman or an important politician.

Messages Written in Blood

The way in which the homicide is committed is only the beginning of the procedure. Hitmen have developed a whole code to communicate among themselves through the homicides that they commit. With the murder, a message tends to be sent; most of the time, it is terrifyingly explicit. For example, the killing is intended to send a warning to the enemy about how vulnerable he or she can be; a corpse covered with a sheet means that the killer knew the victim; mutilating fingers, ears, or the tongue implies that the victim was an informer, a gossip, or a thief. Likewise, dissolving the corpse in acid, known as "cooking it," tends to be reserved for important characters within criminal organizations.

Investigations and interviews conducted in Mexican prisons with more than 270 criminals of varying danger levels, including hired killers for drug-trafficking organizations, reveal statements in which they say that they feel "very proud of doing their job" (Ostrosky, 2012, p. 180). They also consider their acts simply as "going out to work." In the same way, it seems amazing and paradoxical that the same hitmen, who say they have decapitated people, can experience feelings of shame, blushing when they admit they can neither read nor write.

One possible explanation for this contradictory phenomenon is that hitmen are people who are physiologically "underactivated" and consequently they continuously search for novelties and experiences of extreme emotions in their life (Ostrosky, 2012). For example, one of them defined himself as "very crazy" because he used to eat very hot green peppers as sweets: a naive example of this never-ending search for highly stimulating sensations or experiences.

In the same way, it is important to note that, in this "trade," a certain boldness and cunning seems to prevail among hitmen, allowing them to kill in a "quick and clean" way or to commit contemptible acts such as dissolving corpses in acid for just US$600. An example is the case of Santiago Meza López, also known as "el Pozolero," who was captured on January 25, 2009, and who confessed to having "cooked" in acid 300 bodies on the orders of a criminal organization.

From the behavior and personality patterns that hitmen show nowadays, at least three subtypes can be characterized as follows (Ostrosky, 2012):

- *The unsuccessful person:* a person who cannot succeed in a conventional activity because of severe educational and emotional deficiencies. Normally, the person is full of resentment or lacks significant emotional bonds with people who could otherwise help them to achieve gratification through effort and to experience the value of friendship. Therefore, working as a hitman is an escape from becoming a petty criminal.
- *The sadistic person:* a person for whom the trade of being a hitman is a job like any other, allowing him or her to kill without compassion. Sadists enjoy and satisfy themselves by causing harm and provoking suffering in their victims. They have no feelings of guilt; on the contrary, causing pain, hurting others, and destroying fills them with a feeling of pleasure.
- *The dependent person:* a criminal who needs to associate with powerful people and wishes to be recruited, assigned tasks, and distinguished as a "dangerous" individual. As these criminals have a weak personality, they feel best when they are armed and can portray themselves as "fearsome." Consequently, for them, practicing the trade gives identity and meaning to their lives.

Therefore, unlike serial killers or mass murderers, hitmen act fast in a preferably "clean" way and, although they are linked to "bosses," they tend to have little contact with them. In fact, according to their statements, "they are only called when their bosses have to assign them a target to be eliminated" (Ostrosky, 2012, p. 182). In this "working relationship," they use communication codes created by themselves to avoid being understood by people unrelated to the conversation. Often, it is deserters from the Guatemalan army, former Mexican servicemen, and policemen who become hitmen, and they use sophisticated techniques when exercising violence; these are particularly dangerous individuals.

Psychopathy: A Perceptible Fate

Generally, young people who choose the path of crime and delinquency have something in common: in addition to economic inequality and social conflict in their home lives, there is a clear lack of family care and, sometimes, even mistreatment. In recent years, important evidence has shown that individuals who are mistreated during childhood tend to have a higher probability of suffering from mental diseases (e.g. Aebi et al., 2014; Cambron, Gringeri, & Vogel-Ferguson, 2014; Lecic-Tosevski et al., 2014). Some of these studies support the idea that the environment can cause a behavioral change in the long term through epigenetic influence—that is, a modification in gene expression, although not in the DNA sequence, which is caused by external events (e.g. Champagne & Mashoodh, 2009; Miller, 2010; Powledge, 2011).

The economic element is without doubt one of the most attractive factors for becoming a hitman, but unfavorable environments can also lead people into this life (hostile environments, family conflicts, and similar situations). However, there is a particularly important third element: a high percentage of hitmen are psychopaths. Consequently, they are often arrogant, but at the same time charming; they are unable to experience empathy and completely lack feelings of guilt. If they are questioned, pointing out that the people whom they kill are like them, with dreams, children, and desires, they simply reply: "Well, this is my job."

Psychopathic personality is analyzed in more depth in another chapter. However, experiments conducted by the neuroscientist Joshua Buckholtz and collaborators at Vanderbilt University in the United States have driven the theory that the expectation of reward can trigger abnormally high responses in psychopaths' mesolimbic system, releasing four times more dopamine than normal, and creating in them the impulse to seek these extreme stimuli of reward without thinking about the consequences (Buckholtz & Meyer-Lindenberg, 2008; Buckholtz et al., 2010; Kiehl & Buckholtz, 2010). In the opinion of this group of scientists, it could be possible that this impulse to seek out extreme stimuli and the lack of empathy of psychopaths are substantial factors in their predisposition to commit a crime.

A Vicious Circle

Generally, violence within the family is a common element in hitmen. Without access to a proper education and witnessing, and many times suffering from, aggression from their own family in the form of physical violence and insults, the first thing that these young people learn is to hate and then to reproduce the same patterns that they find in their surroundings.

In a study about the effects of exposure to violence in teenagers, Strenziok et al. (2011) selected 29 subjects; these people repeatedly watched videos that displayed varying degrees of aggressive behavior. Skin conductance responses were measured and a downward linear adaptation was found, with increasing aggression and desensitization towards more aggressive videos. The results also revealed an adaptation in a fronto-parietal network including the left lateral orbitofrontal cortex (LOFC), right precuneus, and bilateral inferior parietal lobules, again showing downward linear adaptations and desensitization towards more aggressive videos. Granger causality mapping analyses revealed attenuation in the left LOFC, indicating that activation when viewing aggressive videos is driven by input from parietal regions, which decreased over time with more aggressive videos. It was concluded that aggressive videos activate an emotion–attention network that can blunt emotional responses through reduced attention with repeated viewing, which may restrict the association between the consequences of aggression and an emotional response and, therefore, potentially promote aggressive attitudes and behavior.

The hitman phenomenon is probably the result of multiple factors, including a lack of moral and cultural values; it is also the consequence of socio-economic issues, which mean these young men cannot envision a hopeful future for themselves, grow up on the streets, and see organized crime as the only way out. This "way out" enables them not only to earn a living for themselves and their families, but also to find a sense of belonging, to become "someone," and to gain respect through power and cruelty.

As the products of broken homes, and without the presence of rescuing figures (teachers, psychologists, good friends, or neighbors) or models from whom to learn the fundamental values of life, many of them feel the need to be part of a group, because they are searching for the protection, affection, and respect they do not get at home.

An Example: "El Ponchis," the Young Hitman

In December 2010, a particular criminal case caused great alarm in Mexico. It was the arrest of a young hitman, Édgar Jiménez Lugo, known as "el Ponchis." He was underage and began his criminal career when he was 11 years old. He uploaded videos of the tortures that he inflicted on his victims to YouTube, crimes for which he was financially compensated.

How can a child become a murderer? The first cause is, undoubtedly, of an economic nature. A lack of development at school and in the family home paves the way for two possible paths: despair or vengeance. Important warning signals are the data published by the Consejo Nacional para la Evaluación de la Política de Desarrollo Social (CONEVAL; National Council for the Evaluation of Social Development Policy), which, in 2010, indicated that most Mexicans between 12 and 29 years old live in poverty or vulnerable conditions (CONEVAL, n.d.).

When the aforementioned factors are combined, the result is often catastrophic. The story of "el Ponchis" begins in 1996, in San Diego, California. He was the product of an unwanted and uncontrolled pregnancy, born into a home immersed in domestic violence and to parents who were addicted to alcohol and drugs. The couple, David Antonio Jiménez Solís and Yolanda Jiménez Lugo, had crossed the border into the United States in 1989, taking with them their daughters. Records show that, two years before Édgar was born, his father had been in trouble with the law for acts of domestic violence. Moreover, months before the boy was born, his father was imprisoned for having hit his mother and, during the legal process, he confessed that he inhaled cocaine, smoked marijuana, and drank a pack of beer daily. Even worse than this, his mother admitted that she also inhaled cocaine to improve her mood, even during her pregnancy, because she suffered from depression.

The damage that cocaine can cause while the brain is in development is well documented. For example, in 2006, doctors from Case Western Reserve University found that the children of women who had consumed cocaine during pregnancy showed behavioral problems years later, such as attention deficit disorder (ADD) and oppositional defiant disorder (ODD), as well as a higher level of aggressiveness than that of children who had not had placental contact with the substance (Linares et al., 2006; Singer et al., 2006). Prenatal cocaine exposure has been associated with structural deficits in neonatal cortical gray matter, specifically in prefrontal and frontal regions involved in executive function and inhibitory control (Grewen et al., 2014), as well as with altered response to stress (Chaplin et al., 2014) and an increase in the excitation of dopamine neurons (Hausknecht, Haj-Dahmane, & Shen, 2012).

Édgar lived for only a short time with his mother, until she was arrested for the possession of drugs. At that point, the child was sent to Mexico to live with his maternal grandmother in Jiutepec, Morelos. This change could have been crucial to the child's future. Unfortunately, his grandmother died when Édgar was only 8 years old, leaving him in a state of total abandonment. A child in such a vulnerable situation sometimes finds a "rescuer," whose love, advice, and example can teach the child to channel his or her violence. However, just when he most needed such a person, Édgar lost his grandmother. From then on, the issues in his life would only multiply.

First, he was expelled when he was only in his second year in elementary school, for physically assaulting a girl. Shortly afterwards, when he was about 11 years old, according to him, he was forcibly taken by the leader of a criminal group in the area, Julio de Jesús Radilla, also known as "el Negro," who was related to the drug trade organization of the Beltrán Leyva brothers. However, according to other unconfirmed versions, the child could have been introduced into this environment by one of his sisters, because at that point she was romantically linked to "el Negro." It is not known for certain how he joined the Beltrán Leyva brothers' cartel, but in general the children that join tend to be selected by people within the business. Such children are seen regularly wandering the streets and are given a tempting offer of earning money in exchange for doing a risky, but fast and easy, job.

Professional criminals in this field often start their careers as "falcons," in charge of keeping an eye on something and warning of nearby strangers or police officers. Later, they start to sell drugs on the streets, which normally leads to them consuming the drugs; in very little time, they become trapped by the debts created by their own addiction, with their only exit being to accept any task that is required of them. Of these, one of the most well-paid activities is being a hitman, which brings with it the advantage of giving them certain status in their field. In this way, Édgar ended up being adopted by a violent group who induced him into consuming drugs and encouraged him towards violence, by giving him a form of identity and a sense of belonging. The boy was skillful and cruel; he recorded on his cellphone the tortures that he inflicted on his victims and uploaded the videos to YouTube. For "el Ponchis," boasting of his "accomplishments" was what gave him both fame and misfortune.

He was arrested in December 2010 and, two months later, when he was 14 years old, he was formally accused of cocaine transportation, the possession of firearms that were exclusive to the army, organized crime with the aim of kidnapping, and first-degree murder.

According to some newspaper reports, during his stay in the Center for the Execution of Deprivation of Liberty Measures for Teenagers (CEMPLA, according to its Spanish acronym) in Morelos, Édgar met six other teenagers who had also worked for the Beltrán Leyva cartel, among them another boy younger than 15 years of age, arrested by military men in January 2011. Although Édgar only admits to having worked as a "falcon," he appears in the videos uploaded to the internet.

Reforming "el Ponchis" in the hope of returning him to society will be the greatest challenge that the authority in charge of his case will have to face. This will be a very complex task of rehabilitation, which must include the creation of an affective world for the young man; it is important to retrain him, to allow him to manage his violent impulses, and also to provide him occupational and educational training that allows him to develop himself fully within society.

When an individual lives in a hostile environment, he or she develops aggressive behaviors for defense. However, if a child lives in a constant state of abandonment, risk, and threat, these aggressive behaviors may be permanently established. Unfortunately, the story of "el Ponchis" is the sad reality of many other young Mexican people, for whom death has become a trivial component—a sort of routine that forms part of their everyday lives. According to the *Global Report on Violence Against Children* supported by UNICEF (Pinheiro, 2006), every day two children younger than 14 years of age die in Mexico as a result of violence.

References

Aebi, M., Linhart, S., Thun-Hohenstein, L., Bessler, C., Steinhausen, H.C., & Plattner, B. (2014). Detained male adolescent offender's emotional, physical and sexual maltreatment profiles and their associations to psychiatric disorders and criminal behaviors. *Journal of Abnormal Child Psychology*, 43(5), 1–11.

Buckholtz, J.W., & Meyer-Lindenberg, A. (2008). MAOA and the neurogenetic architecture of human aggression. *Trends in Neurosciences*, 31(3), 120–129.

Buckholtz, J.W., Treadway, M.T., Cowan, R.L., Woodward, N.D., Benning, S.D., Li, R., ... & Zald, D.H. (2010). Mesolimbic dopamine reward system hypersensitivity in individuals with psychopathic traits. *Nature Neuroscience*, 13(4), 419–421.

Cambron, C., Gringeri, C., & Vogel-Ferguson, M.B. (2014). Physical and mental health correlates of adverse childhood experiences among low-income women. *Health & Social Work*, 39(4), 221–229.

Champagne, F.A., & Mashoodh, R. (2009). Genes in context gene–environment interplay and the origins of individual differences in behavior. *Current Directions in Psychological Science*, 18(3), 127–131.

Chaplin, T.M., Visconti, K.J., Molfese, P.J., Susman, E.J., Klein, L.C., Sinha, R., & Mayes, L.C. (2014). Prenatal cocaine exposure differentially affects stress responses in girls and boys: Associations with future substance use. *Development and Psychopathology*, 27(1), 163–180.

CONEVAL, (n.d.). Retrieved on June 6, 2015 from: www.coneval.gob.mx/Paginas/principal.aspx.

Grewen, K., Burchinal, M., Vachet, C., Gouttard, S., Gilmore, J.H., Lin, W., ... & Gerig, G. (2014). Prenatal cocaine effects on brain structure in early infancy. *NeuroImage*, 101(1), 114–123.

Hausknecht, K., Haj-Dahmane, S., & Shen, R.Y. (2012). Prenatal stress exposure increases the excitation of dopamine neurons in the ventral tegmental area and alters their responses to psychostimulants. *Neuropsychopharmacology*, 38(2), 293–301.

Kiehl, K.A., & Buckholtz, J.W. (2010). Inside the mind of a psychopath. *Scientific American Mind*, 21(4), 22–29.

Lecic-Tosevski, D., Draganic-Gajic, S., Pejovic-Milovancevic, M., Popovic-Deusic, S., Christodoulou, N., & Botbol, M. (2014). Child is father of the man: Child abuse and development of future psychopathology. *Psychiatriki*, 25(3), 185–191.

Linares, T.J., Singer, L.T., Kirchner, H.L., Short, E.J., Min, M.O., Hussey, P., & Minnes, S. (2006). Mental health outcomes of cocaine-exposed children at 6 years of age. *Journal of Pediatric Psychology*, 31(1), 85–97.

Miller, G. (2010). The seductive allure of behavioral epigenetics. *Science*, 329(5987), 24–27.

Ostrosky, F. (2012). *Mentes Asesinos: La Violenca en Tu Cerebro* [*Criminal Minds: The Violence in Your Brain*]. Mexico City: Quinto Sol.

Ostrosky, F., Borja, K.C., Rebollar, C.R., & Díaz Galván, K.X. (2011). Neuropsychological profiles of members of organized crime and drug-traffic organizations. *Research and Reports in Forensic Medical Science*, 2, 19–30.

Pinheiro, P.S. (2006). *Informe Mundial Sobre la Violencia Contra los Niños y Niñas* [*Global Report on Violence Against Children*]. Geneva, Switzerland: ONU.

Powledge, T. (2011). Behavioral epigenetics: How nurture shapes nature. *BioScience*, 61(8), 588–592.

Singer, L.T., Lewin, J., Minnes, S., Weishampel, P., Drake, K., Satayathum, S., ... & Evans, A. (2006). Neuroimaging of 7–8-year-old children exposed prenatally to cocaine. *Neurotoxicology and Teratology*, 28(3), 386–402.

Strenziok, M., Krueger, F., Deshpande, G., Lenroot, R.K., van der Meer, E., & Grafman, J. (2011). Fronto-parietal regulation of media violence exposure in adolescents: A multi-method study. *Social Cognitive and Affective Neuroscience*, 6(5), 537–547.

9

PARAMILITARISM IN COLOMBIA

Fernando Díaz Colorado[1]

Defining Paramilitarism

The term "paramilitarism" has been defined differently by the various authors that have undertaken its study. While some of these authors have defined paramilitarism as the exercising of violence by criminal groups, such as urban or rural militias, death squads, self-defense forces, or local watchmen (Campbell, 2000; Cubides, 1999; Huggins, 1991; Manitzas, 1991; Warren, 1998), others have described it as an association between irregular groups and some members of a State's armed forces, seeking to fight the threat and subversion of organized crime. However different these views are, there is complete agreement between authors on the facts that the actions conducted by paramilitary groups are illegal or an abuse of power, and that the objective of such groups is the defense of individual, political, or corrupt interests.

From a theoretical perspective, Kalivas and Arjona (as cited in Rangel, 2007) have suggested that "paramilitary forces are armed groups formed outside of a State's formal structure. Nonetheless, they are directly or indirectly associated with it and its local agents, or otherwise tolerated by it" (p. 29). As we can see, defining paramilitarism is not a simple task. Given that it is a multifaceted and complex issue, with political, military, anthropological, and sociological connotations, there is no unanimity in its definition.

From an etiological standpoint, it can be argued that paramilitarism is not such a recent phenomenon as is usually assumed. According to Robin (2003), the French were the first to employ paramilitary organizations as a strategy for consolidating their colonialist and repressive authority over independence movements in both Indochina and Algeria. The counter-revolutionary struggle model established by the French military was founded with the purpose of gaining the support and submission of the population, through the elimination of all actions that countered and opposed colonialist interests.

The French military sought to fulfill this purpose through war techniques and the formation of death squads. This led to a pattern that had many similarities to the model of the Battle of Algiers, which was first taught at the Post-War School of Paris in 1958. Subsequently, it was adopted by the Escuela Superior de Guerra de Buenos Aires (Buenos Aires High School of War) in Argentina and the School of the Americas in the United States, where Latin American military officers were trained. As a consequence, death squads were formed in Central and South American countries such as Panama, the Dominican Republic, Nicaragua, El Salvador, Mexico, Argentina, Brazil, Costa Rica, Guatemala, Venezuela, Bolivia, and Uruguay to support both the dictatorships and the counter-revolutionary struggles, based on ideas that emerged from the Cold War, advocating the fight against every movement that was considered leftist or perceived as promoting communist notions (Velásquez, 2007).

In a broad sense, paramilitarism can be understood as a group of organizations that do not legally or legitimately belong to a State's armed forces, but have a structure and disciplinary model that is similar to the army's. These types of organizations can sometimes be of service to the interests of the State, groups in power, or criminal bands, but they are generally outside the scope of the law.

Overall, paramilitary groups do not obey national or international war conventions, treaties, or agreements, such as international humanitarian law. This leads them to commit serious criminal acts against humanity that include forced displacement, massacres, planting of antipersonnel landmines, enforced disappearances, selective murders, public executions, kidnappings, torture, sexual violence, slavery, mass sterilization, and extensive persecution.

A friend–enemy rationale supports the actions of paramilitary groups. This rationale deems that people who do not share their beliefs, purposes, and objectives must be eliminated. From this perspective, the aim of paramilitary groups is the use of both violence and fear to win a war and destroy the enemy, as well as the achievement of full submission, obedience, and control over the territories in which they operate.

From a different perspective, some academics have described the perverse actions of paramilitary groups as terrorism. However, given the ambiguity and the diversity of views that have developed around the subject, attempting to conceptualize terrorism is not an easy task. For most of the academics who have undertaken its study, terrorism is related to an excessive use of violence that seeks to create fear and panic in the population, with a final objective of subduing the current legal and legitimate power and thus exposing the State's fragility or inability to ensure safety for its inhabitants. According to Rementería (2009), terrorism is the use of maximum destructive capacity against an unarmed population. It is the highest form of violence, where pain is inflicted to subdue the other's will. Terrorism involves murdering people who do not have the means to defend themselves or the opportunity to surrender. Moreover, Hoffman (2003) suggests that an essential characteristic of terrorist actions is that violence is planned, calculated, and conducted in a systematic manner for an eminently political objective.

Wieviorka (1991) has noted that terrorism is a threat that involves the negation of the social nexus. For this reason, terrorism has to be viewed in the context of the social conditions in which it occurs, in order to understand the reasons behind actions aimed at destroying the existing social order. In this sense, terrorism is a political weapon that intends to destroy a form of society that is not compatible with the terrorists' views. Since their objective is to enforce fear, take control, and exert power over the population, paramilitary groups identify with terrorist groups. As a consequence, various paramilitary actions can be the same as terrorist actions, although they do not necessarily share the same objectives. Furthermore, it is worth noting that the association between paramilitary groups and a country's armed forces is considered State terrorism (Hoffman, 2003). However, regardless of the definition of terrorism, there is no doubt that its actions produce a collective trauma that involves both an impact on the basic social structure and damage to a community's bonds, thereby undermining its prevailing beliefs (Erickson, 1994).

The Origins of Paramilitarism in Colombia

As we have seen so far, paramilitarism is the exercise of systematic violence. Hence, it creates and/or leads to terror, fear, social paralysis, domination, and submission, all of which are, without doubt, the same means used by terrorist groups. Nonetheless, in Colombia, the aim of paramilitarism is not to achieve political objectives, but rather to strengthen the power of the paramilitary group by creating alliances with corrupt political groups. This allows paramilitary forces to broaden their local and regional power, thereby extending their criminal businesses and hampering the actions of the judicial system. As noted in the research conducted by Maya (2012), paramilitary groups intend to consolidate a corrupt alliance between drug traffickers, politicians, and private and public companies to allow their organized criminal activity free rein. In other words, their fundamental purpose is the consolidation of a corrupt structure within local governments, with the support of local, regional, and national politicians, and government officials from municipal councils, departmental assemblies, and Congress.

In Colombia, diverse interpretations and definitions of paramilitarism have developed in different contexts. Definitions have been developed by the government (illegal self-defense), police forces (private justice groups or militias), and academia (illegal armies, criminal bands, armies serving organized crime, or subversive groups). Despite the differences between these definitions, there is agreement regarding the definition of illegal armed groups in Colombia. These include guerilla groups, militias, drug-trafficking and organized crime gangs, private armies, death squads with social cleansing purposes, and, finally, armed groups of a rightist ideology that combat guerillas. These right-wing armed groups defend the interests of organized crime gangs, mainly drug traffickers, and have close cooperative links with State employees, as well as with members of the military forces, the police, and political parties with local, regional, and national influence.

The origins of paramilitarism in Colombia can be located in the mid-twentieth century. During this period, violence increased, with the forming of criminal groups such as "pájaros"[2] and "chulavitas."[3] These groups defended different economic and political interests, leading to an armed confrontation between the traditional liberal and conservative political parties. Moreover, these criminal groups acted with complicity from local and police authorities in murdering opponents, setting fires, stealing, and forcibly displacing the population (Guzmán, Fals, & Umaña, 1998).

However, it appears that the formal appearance of armed groups operating outside the Colombian State's control took place between 1965 and 1968, as a result of Law 48 and Decree 3398. These official orders laid the legal foundations that allowed for the creation of civil defense organizations operating against the actions of guerillas and malefactors in Colombian territories. Initially, these organizations were called rural self-defense forces. Subsequently, private cooperatives, known as "Convivir," were developed with the objective of providing security to some of the country's territories. Finally, paramilitary groups were formed.

One of the main groups, the Autodefensas Unidas de Colombia (AUC; United Self-Defense Forces of Colombia), was formed at the beginning of the 1980s, as a result of a coalition between private armies of rightist ideologies. These armies used the armed conflict between the State and the guerillas to disguise their illicit economic activities, which included drug trafficking, forced displacement, kidnapping, and extortion. The AUC came to operate in two-thirds of the country, with nearly 30,000 combatants. Numerous members of the AUC infiltrated the State's establishments and political parties, until it achieved a significant representation in Congress (Ronderos, 2014).

It is important to highlight that paramilitary groups have received economic and logistic support from multinational companies, such as Chiquita Brands, Nestlé, Drummond, and Prodeco, a subsidiary of Glencore. This is outlined in a report entitled *The Dark Side of Coal: Paramilitary Violence in the Cesar Region, Colombia* (PAX, 2014). The report presents testimonies from demobilized paramilitaries, former employees of the aforementioned companies, and victims of the conflict that took place between 1996 and 2006, when paramilitary groups had control over the department of Cesar. The testimonies suggest that, during this period of time, coordinated actions took place between paramilitary groups, members of the State's military intelligence, and the departments of security of the cited companies. These coordinated actions involved both economic contribution from and the support of these multinational companies for the implementation of activities that were aimed at fighting, reporting, and highlighting union members and others who were suspected of being part of the guerilla groups.

This perverse alliance was beneficial for all of those involved. As a result of the forced displacement of native people who fled from their territories following the violence exerted by paramilitary groups, the multinational companies managed to illegally acquire extensive grounds that were rich in coal and mineral resources.

How Paramilitary Groups Operated

These paramilitary groups were armed groups, with between 10 and 150 combatants. Some parts of such organizations operated as death squads, moving in smaller units to avoid detection, systematically eliminating their enemies, and creating fear in the local population. Other parts of these organizations worked in larger groups and in a military fashion to expel their enemies from their territories by using "cutting and burning" tactics (Dudley, 2008).

Although it appears that such paramilitary groups sought to fight the guerillas, their principal activity was the control of the drug-trafficking corridors and the protection of the regions where coca was cultivated and cocaine processed. The main drug traffickers were involved in funding and leading the paramilitary groups in the country, but their presence was especially relevant in the region of Magdalena Medio, in the north-east of the department of Antioquia, and the departments of Córdoba and Meta. The AUC was thus concentrated on areas of the country that were considered of major economic and strategic interest, such as Cesar, La Guajira, Magdalena, Atlántico, Bolívar, Sucre, Córdoba, Antioquia, Caldas, Risaralda, Chocó, Tolima, Valle del Cauca, Cauca, Nariño, Putumayo, Caquetá, Guaviare, Meta, Vichada, Casanare, Arauca, Cundinamarca, Boyacá, Santander, and Norte de Santander (Human Rights Watch, 2001).

The Barbarity of Paramilitarism

Let us now take a look at some figures that give an idea of the scale of the barbarity that was experienced in Colombia as a result of the armed conflict. According to a report developed by the Centro Nacional de Memoria Histórica (National Center for Historical Memory; 2010), the internal war in Colombia caused 218,094 deaths between 1958 and 2012. Moreover, 1,962 massacres were committed between 1980 and 2012, of which 1,166 were perpetrated by paramilitary groups, 343 by the guerillas, and 158 by the security services (295 were committed by unidentified groups). In addition, more than three million people were forcibly displaced and numerous civilian victims were maimed by the antipersonnel landmines that were planted in the majority of the national territory.

The fear and terror that were inflicted by the paramilitaries taking over people's territories were part of a strategy to control the population and dismantle its social organizations through the dramatization of violence (mutilated bodies were exhibited, collective or individual public executions were conducted, etc.). Paramilitary groups intimidated the population to inhibit social action, inflicted terror to paralyze communities, and caused fear to give the paramilitary objectives free rein. Hence, most massacres were conducted not only to eliminate their victims, but also to incite fear in spectators (Blair, 2001; Correa & Rueda, 2002; Duque, 2009).

The dismemberment of living people became common practice among paramilitary groups. The shattering of bodies using a machete or a chainsaw served three purposes. First, it killed the victim and made him or her disappear, both physically and symbolically. Second, it established an initiation ritual that removed recently admitted and young combatants' sensibilities. Third, it made the sanguinary and heavy job of disposing of the corpse quicker and easier by reducing the physical effort required to dig the grave, since it was recognized that, when a body was cut up into small pieces, a grave of approximately 60 centimeters deep was sufficient (Revista Semana, 2007a). Social scientists have conducted research on the interpretation of violent deaths in Colombia and the destruction of the body as a recurring action of violence. This research has been mainly approached from anthropological and sociological perspectives.

From a psychological perspective, on the other hand, research on this subject has been carried out with demobilized combatants and victims of the armed conflict. It has also involved the analysis of declarations and statements given by defectors and detained members of paramilitaries to the authorities. In addition, the issue has been approached from a psychoanalytical perspective (Blair, 2001; Castro, 2002; Díaz, 2002; Uribe, 1990). The study of this subject constitutes a significant challenge for the psychological discipline in Colombia. The scientific research that has been produced is scarce and lacks the explicative power that is required to fully comprehend the psychology of the members of the guerilla groups, paramilitary forces, and organized crime gangs.

The Massacres Committed by Paramilitary Groups

For some authors, a massacre is a form of collective violence committed against vulnerable people who cannot escape or resist it, or an excessive action where violence has absolute freedom (Sofsky, 1998, as cited in Blair, 2001). For other authors, such as Suarez and Martínez (2009), a massacre is the intentional homicide of four or more people who are in a state of vulnerability and in the same time, manner, and place. Uribe (2004) defines it as the collective murder of unarmed and vulnerable people that is committed by an armed group, and Uribe and Vásquez (1995) defines it as the violent act of physically eliminating four or more vulnerable people simultaneously or quasi-simultaneously.

According to Colorado et al. (2008), Colombia is a violent social construction in which massacres have reflected social and political issues surrounding a fight that is based on the annihilation of the opposition. This same author suggests that Colombia has experienced not only a war of battles, but also a war of massacres that reflects both the degradation of the war and the disdain of the combatants towards civil society. In this war, there is an evident and significant relationship between the body and violence that, although it is not the only aspect, has been widely explored in the analysis of violence (Blair, 2001; Súarez & Martínez, 2009; Uribe 1990, 2004; Uribe & Vásquez, 1995). Furthermore, Uribe (2004) notes that, in the middle of the twentieth century, some of the acts of violence perpetrated by the "chulavitas" involved torturing victims in multiple ways prior to their execution. All of this affected their relatives and family members, who were forced to witness the abuses and violence or were rubbed with the body parts of the victims. The most frequent forms of torture were tying victims' arms behind their backs, cutting them with the blade of a machete until they bled out slowly, and sexually abusing women in front of men.

The paramilitaries used the word *porqueriza* to refer to a place that they frequently chose to massacre their victims. The places chosen have some similarities with the places chosen for breeding and sacrificing animals. The murdered bodies were left in these places, and some people were left there to bleed to death. In other words, the paramilitaries followed a very similar procedure to the one employed by butchers in slaughterhouses for cattle and pigs (Uribe, 2004).

Ultimately, a massacre involves more than an act of murder. It is the ultimate expression of excess and barbarity. According to Blair (2001), death as the result of a "clean" homicide does not have the same meaning as death as a result of a murder committed in a brutal and treacherous way. Neither is a death that ends with a person's physical passing the same as one that involves mutilations of the body, as the latter is, in some way, symbolic and a messenger of terror. The latter is excessive and committed through actions that are loaded with meaning: not just one bullet, but 20; not just death, but maiming and death.

As we can see, massacres have frequently occurred throughout Colombian history. They have been a constant in the expression of violence and the systematic inciting of terror. Sargent Florencio Jiménez committed one of the better-known massacres, on August 17, 1830. He murdered the prisoners of the Battle of El Santuario during the time of independence. At the beginning of the twentieth century, the victims of the Thousand Days' War amounted to 100,000. Moreover, one of the most unfortunate events in Colombia's history took place on May 10, 1909, when 60 indigenous people were incinerated by the company Arana Hermanos, which considered them its slaves (Uribe, 2004). In addition, on December 6, 1928, a general strike organized by the workers' union of the United Fruit Company ended in the Banana Massacre: the murder of 1,500 workers ordered by General Carlos Cortés Vargas. Thereafter, in 1952, a group of soldiers in Armero, Tolima, forced 60 farmers to lock themselves inside a barn that was later burned down by the troops. That same year, the Tolima battalion committed one of the most devastating massacres in the municipality of Líbano, where approximately 1,500 murders were committed (Pinto, 1989). Additionally, in the village of San Pablo, located in the municipality of Cunday, troops forced

140 liberal men to march in single file to the municipality of Villarica, where they were all murdered. A decade later, the killings of the bandits known as "Desquite," "Chispas," "Sangrenegra," and "Tarzán" took place. They ravaged entire regions, killing men, women, children, and the elderly. Later, in the 1970s, the settlers of the Llanos Orientales territory massacred the "Cuibas" indigenous people.

The Body as a Device for Vengeance

According to Gonzáles (2011), violence in Colombia is systematically and generally exerted against the civil population. Killings are committed either individually or collectively, and violence is conducted in a sadistic, horrifying, and ritualistic manner. Children are beheaded in front of their parents; victims' eyes and internal organs are torn from their bodies in punishment or to "do justice." Behind these horrors is not war, but a hatred that is transmitted from one generation to another. In Colombia, vengeance and hatred are transmitted from parents to children, along with loyalty to the death and disgust for enemies.

One of the most commonly recurring violent behaviors in Colombia has been the use of the body as a device for vengeance, humiliation, and disdain for the enemy. In Colombia, murdering the enemy does not resolve a conflict. The body becomes the recipient of acts that allow the enemy to satisfy a desire for vengeance or to carry out an idea of justice. It thus has to be broken, dismembered, chopped up, and profaned to demonstrate the worthlessness of the enemy, who is considered a subject of lesser value and inferior condition.

According to the concept of "enemy" suggested by Schmitt (as cited in Mouffe, 1999), it can be argued that a friend–enemy distinction[4] has been drawn in the Colombian conflict. This distinction entails a need to completely demolish your adversary. Rivalry is thus not something that is admitted to in Colombia; instead, the concept of enemies is preferred. Since coexistence is not considered possible, someone has to disappear and the enemy has to be eliminated. Furthermore, Uribe (2004), an anthropologist who studied the violence that took place during the 1950s, notes that Colombians have been incapable of mourning death. However, the only difference between the violence seen in the 1950s and the violence that the country is currently experiencing is the sophistication of the weapons. While machetes were used then, chainsaws and high-accuracy rifles are now preferred. Moreover, although 60% of the country was rural in the 1950s, there has been no improvement in rural violence, despite that proportion now being smaller; the modernization of instruments of war has made killing much more effective.

Throughout Colombian history, murders have been brutal, involving maiming and leaving unrecognizable the victim. It is not considered enough to shoot a man; he has to be castrated, beheaded, and have his hands cut off. This type of cruelty is an inherent characteristic of the human species. It was experienced in Rwanda,

Africa, and in Germany by the Nazis, but in Colombia dismemberment practices persist and bodies are cut up into small pieces to make them fit in small spaces. As Sofsky (1998, as cited in Blair, 2001) argues, perpetrators tend to display an eagerness to mutilate corpses, seeing it as a way of killing the dead for a second time. The killers work closely and with their hands. They want to be able to see the body bleeding and the fearful eyes of the victim. Committing a massacre places no pressure on the perpetrators, who do not display any fear, shame, or guilt. Thus, a massacre not only leaves ruins, ashes, and many deaths in its trail, but also destroys life, order, and culture. Mutilating and destroying the body can be understood as the best way of despising and devaluing the enemy, and of communicating the power of the perpetrator.

By the middle of the twentieth century, rituals had developed in massacre and dismemberment practices in Colombia. Perpetrators took their time, quartering their victims and laying their body parts in unnatural positions. For example, they placed the head between the legs of the victims or the penis in the mouth. There was therefore an intention to cause terror, which was also achieved through the dismemberment of living people. No clear explanation has been found for these actions, and Colombia has experienced an inconceivable amount of pain and has witnessed barbaric acts that are not seen anywhere else in the continent.

Testimonies of the Barbarity of Paramilitarism

Some of the commandants and members of the illegal self-defense groups have now confessed to the execution of numerous killings in different areas of the national territory. They have done so within the legal framework of the Ley de Justicia y Paz (Justice and Peace Law), which was developed by Colombia's former president Álvaro Uribe Velez to deal with members of paramilitary groups. Their testimonies discuss how learning to kill the enemy became a paramilitary practice and recruits received training on dismembering living people. This was known as a test of courage; therefore, in this context, dying was not the problem— it was being killed (Pinto, 1989).

Francisco Enrique Villalba Hernández, known as Cristian Barreto, was one of the paramilitary members who received this type of training. He was taught to handle weapons and manufacture homemade bombs and was later one of the perpetrators of the "El Aro" massacre in Ituango, Antioquia. While detained in La Picota prison in Bogotá, he provided a detailed description of the orders he followed. He recounted being sent to participate in a training course at a farm called La 35 in El Tomate, Antioquia, in 1994. During his time on this training course, his day began at 5 am and he received direct instructions from high commanders, such as "Doble Cero" ("Double Zero"). Villalba reported learning and practicing dismemberment on local farmers when the paramilitaries took over their towns. They were mostly elderly people and they were tied up, transported in trucks, and taken to a room where they remained confined for a few days or until the training started. They were then dragged from the room in their underwear and taken to the place where the instructor was waiting to give his first instructions. These included cutting off their arms and heads, as well as dismembering them alive. During the test of courage, the trainees were divided into four or five groups to dismember the farmers. The instructor guided each trainee in a group and reassured them of their actions. Villalba noted that the paramilitary members following these orders needed reassurance when dismembering someone, as the victims would often cry out and ask them for mercy (Torres, 2006).

When describing the dismemberment process, Villalba said that they opened the victims from their chests through their stomachs and used their hands to pull out their guts. Then, they cut off their legs, arms, and head using a knife or machete. This was the test of courage for the trainees and was intended to teach them how to kill a person. Villalba recounted an incident were one of the trainees refused to perform the dismemberment and "Doble Cero" stood up and showed him how to do it. He then ordered the other trainees to dismember the one who refused.

During the month and a half that Villalba participated in the course, he witnessed the dismemberment instructions being given three times. The instructors chose which trainees were to participate, and one time he was ordered to cut off the arm of a girl whose leg had already been removed. She begged him not to do it and said she had two children. But her body was taken, along with the others, to the graves on the farm, where it is calculated that more than 400 people were buried (Torres, 2006).

In addition to this account, an informant contacted a group of investigators of the Colombian Prosecution Office to report how various military chiefs, who operated in the departments of Cordoba and Sucre, started building artificial lakes on their farms. According to the informant, people from the area warned the engineers that, by building the artificial lakes, they were contributing to the concealment of mass graves. One of the investigators said that, while this report was an indication of a possible crime, a couple of the artificial lakes needed to be drained to find evidence. He added that confirming this crime would explain why farms that were used as paramilitary killing fields, such as El Palmar, had caimans and alligators. Furthermore, Cepeda, a researcher on human rights violations, has asserted that various witnesses informed him of several bodies that were devoured by caimans. These events are reported as being widespread in the city of Mompox, on a farm owned by the paramilitary commandant "Chepe Barrera" (Torres, 2006).

Furthermore, the Colombian Prosecution Office has found 43 skeletal remains on the El Palmar farm since the excavations began in 2005. This is the biggest farm in the municipality of San Onofre, which is located in the department of Sucre, and it is estimated that the remains of around 300 people are still hidden in various places throughout the farm. It is also believed that many inhabitants of this municipality are buried there, because people who were taken to El Palmar never got out alive and the location of their graves is still unknown. The remains found so far are a result of the testimonies of paramilitary massacre executioners who made the decision to speak to the prosecution. Some victims were buried in mass graves that were located further away from the farm houses. One of these farm houses had a room that was known as the "room of the last tear," where, according to an inhabitant of San Onofre, victims were tortured and humiliated. The few people who survived were taken to a tree on the farm, where they were hung and quartered like cattle, so that they would fit into small graves. Of the 36 graves found in 2005, only one had the remains of four people. The rest were individual graves of 80 to 120 centimeters deep and a diameter of 120 inches (Arcieri, 2007). A year after the authorities started to excavate the graves, horrifying information started to be revealed of the paramilitaries giving lessons on how to dismember their victims. The Aguilas Negras (Black Eagles) group dug up their bodies and threw them into rivers to prevent them from being found.

After the first year of excavations and since April 2007, the Colombian Prosecution Office has received 3,710 reports of probable locations of mass graves, but most of these have not been explored due to a lack of resources. Although 533 bodies have been found, only 13 have been completely identified through DNA tests and 173 have been preliminarily identified through individual marks or items such as clothes, tattoos, etc.[5]

The paramilitaries' testimonies and the results of forensic teams' investigations have led to the conclusion that the AUC not only designed a method for dismembering human beings, but also gave lessons on how to do so by using living people who were taken to their training fields. As mentioned above, Villalba revealed details of these lessons and reported that the victims were elderly people who were transported in trucks with their arms tied behind their backs. Paramilitary trainees were then dispatched in groups of five and received instructions on how to cut off the victims' arms and heads and dismember them alive.

Chainsaws do not appear to have been used on most of the bodies that have been exhumed so far. According to a prosecutor who specializes in exhumations, machetes were preferred over chainsaws, as the latter were considered unpractical because they could easily become tangled in the victims' clothes. Hence, 70% of the bodies that have been exhumed on the north coast of Colombia were dismembered with a machete. Moreover, the majority of the bodies that were found in Putumayo, to which Carlos Castaño first transferred his death machinery from Urabá and Córdoba, received a shot to the head and were later dismembered, cut at every prominent joint (Arcieri, 2007).

The testimony of "Relámpago," a former paramilitary member who worked in the service of Fidel Castaño, one of the founders of paramilitarism, shows the barbarity of paramilitary actions. He recounted seeing a boy who not only had his ears and genitals cut off, but also had his eyes pushed in until he was left blind. Even then, he begged his persecutors to let him live, but a few minutes later a bullet ended his life. In addition, "Relámpago" confessed that paramilitaries hung people before shooting them. While one of his peers pulled the rope, the other hung onto the victim's legs. For paramilitaries, death without torture was considered a concession that was granted only to children and women (Revista Semana, 1990).

However, the question remains: why did paramilitaries dismember their victims? The explanation seems to lie in a gruesome pragmatism. Paramilitaries had to bury their victims to reduce their risks of being put on trial by national and international judges for committing crimes against humanity and so, to save energy and to avoid having to dig deep graves, it was considered best to dismember the bodies. A commander of paramilitary groups in Los Llanos explained that the holes were dug according to the measurements of the trunk of the victims' bodies. He said that it was a job that could be done in ten minutes by four or five women. Consequently, there does not seem to be an anthropological explanation for wanting to hide the victims; it was just a practical solution (Arcieri, 2007).

One of the paramilitary chiefs, Salvatore Mancuso, confessed that, to prevent the authorities from finding the body of the indigenous leader Kimi Pernía, it was taken out of its original grave and thrown into the Sinú River. To hide his crimes, Mancuso ordered bodies to be exhumed from a farm in San José de Ralito, where his group had buried various bodies.

Massacre as a Strategy for Territorial Domination

With the intensification of violence in Colombia, long-established criminal methods are being used. Massacres have been committed in a context in which violence is considered business. According to Corredor (1990), massacres have often been connected to Colombian agrarian history, and such instances can be split into four specific time periods. First, there were the agrarian conflicts of the 1930s, in which important rural actors guined access to land through invasion. Second, there was the violence of the 1940s and 1950s, which resulted in a reorganization of properties and previous landowners recovering the lands that the farmers had illegally acquired. Third, there were the massive invasions of land that took place in the 1970s. Finally, there was the intensive escalation of violence in the rural sector that, taking the form of genocide, caused the displacement and eviction of farmers during the 1980s and 1990s.

As well as this, the violent dimensions that drug trafficking has been gaining since 1984 have caused an increase in genocidal practices in rural areas of the country. The violence connected to drug trafficking was the result of similar factors as the violence that resulted from landowners' intentions of exacting revenge in those areas where farmers had invaded their lands and agrarian conflicts had occurred in the previous decade. Through hired gunmen, landlords committed massacres and obtained revenge, while, in turn, drug traffickers managed to become landowners.

By achieving this economic purpose, drug traffickers also fulfilled their political objective of reducing the guerillas' social support through the generation of terror. According to Gonzáles (2011), the guerillas and drug traffickers were agents of a distinct colonizing dynamic and, thus, became sociopolitical and economic alternatives for a community that lacked both a proper communication channel with the organizations of the State and a process for institutional reintegration. Moreover, the fight for territorial domination that took place between the guerilla groups and the paramilitaries in Colombia led to the forced displacement of more than three million people. The main methods that were used to take control over territories were murders and massacres (Aranguren, 2002). In Urabá, for example, these armed groups conducted six massacres in 1995 in which 86 people were killed. In addition, 952 massacres committed by fewer than five individuals were seen in one case.

The series of massacres began after the Fuerzas Armadas Revolucionarias de Colombia (FARC; Revolutionary Armed Forces of Colombia) guerilla group murdered six people in the municipality of Apartadó, two of whom were soldiers dressed as civilians. The paramilitaries responded by massacring 18 people in a nightclub in a neighborhood inhabited by various members of the political party Unión Patriótica (Patriotic Union), which was considered the political wing of the guerillas. Thereon in, vengeance and massacres became a continuous and useful practice for illegal organizations. This led to the formation of armies that were willing to eliminate everything and everyone suspected of association with the enemy. The business of death began to operate in an incontrollable manner. The deceased paramilitary leader Carlos Castaño said that 50% of the members of the self-defense groups understood war as a way of living and many commandants were only interested in the money (Aranguren, 2002).

Possible Explanations

Investigating the psychology of paramilitary members, the views they have of the world, and the meanings they give to massacre and torture practices is a task long overdue for Colombian psychologists. It appears that the most horrible crimes committed by men have been the product not of mental illnesses or disorders, but of clearly defined and carefully thought-out reasons. From a psychological perspective, human beings' first reaction to suffering violence, experiencing an outrage, or feeling in danger is to protect and defend themselves. This reaction is either voluntary or involuntary, and is accompanied by an emotional outburst that can range from crying to seeking vengeance. Thus, the individual affected by aggression tends to seek justice, restoration, and revenge, to a point where this desire can sometimes become a fundamental imperative that gives meaning to his or her existence. Vengeance makes the person an instrument of passion. During a long wait for revenge, and through repetitive thoughts and calculations, an intense desire arises to destroy the enemy to achieve satisfaction. When a murder takes place, the avenger usually identifies with the victim, wanting to restore his or her worth and repair the harm that was caused. But the avenger is incapable of mourning the death and therefore becomes a victim him- or herself, giving way to vengeance and a never-ending cycle of violence.

In an attempt to explain the horror of paramilitary massacres, it has been argued that their basis is the hatred felt towards people who are either political opponents and guerilla supporters or not considered worthy of living because they are thieves, drug addicts, or homosexuals. As suggested by the Canadian historian Michael Ignatieff (1999), there is no war more savage than a civil war, no crime more violent than fratricide, and no hatred more implacable than that between close relatives. Ideology, interests, and the desire to exert power enhance hatred. The perception of the enemy as unworthy, inferior, and unequal facilitates the execution of atrocities. In the perpetrator's eyes, the victim is not being executed, but is a human being who does not deserve to live.

Hatred is also a feeling fed by prejudices and legitimized through power. It serves as an explanation for practices such as torture, which has not always been an instrument for obtaining information, but often a way to maximize the degradation of the victims. A similar analysis can be applied to sexual violence against women, a practice that injures both their bodies and their dignities. Moreover, lasting damage is done when the victims' bodies are hidden. Where there is no body, mourning cannot take place and, without mourning, a vast hole is created in the soul of society. Unburied corpses are thus a Colombian collective trauma that has been difficult to overcome (Revista Semana, 2007b).

Paramilitary Chiefs and Their Crimes

Salvatore Mancuso has been charged with 932 enforced disappearances, 1,295 forced displacements, 175 offenses of gender-based violence, and 150 illegal recruitments. In addition, he is accused of having committed the massacres and displacements that occurred in the municipalities of Las Palmas and Montes de María in 1999, and El Salado and Carmen de Bolivar in 2000. He is also accused of more than 62 homicides.

Julián Bolivar has been charged with 336 enforced disappearances, 572 forced displacements, 173 offenses of gender-based violence, and 52 illegal recruitments. In addition, he is accused of having committed multiple homicides and using torture techniques.

Ramiro Vanoy (known as "Cuco") is accused of having committed 108 enforced disappearances, 62 forced displacements, 14 offenses of gender-based violence, and 27 illegal recruitments. He is also considered responsible for the massacre of "Juntas" in Puerto Valdivia, Antioquia, and the massacres of "La Granja" and "El Aro" in 1996.

Diego Murillo (commonly known as "Don Berna") is accused of having committed 85 enforced disappearances, 805 forced displacements, 31 offenses of gender-based violence, and 64 illegal recruitments. In addition, he is considered responsible for the massacre of "El Pedregal" in the city of Medellin in 2001, as well as for the massacre of San Jose de Apartadó in 2005.

Ramón Isaza is accused of having committed 314 enforced disappearances, 389 forced displacements, 32 offenses of gender-based violence, and 84 illegal recruitments. He is also considered responsible for the massacre of "Esperanza" in the municipality of Carmen de Viboral in 1996, as well as for the forced displacement of trade unionists in 2002.

Arnubio Triana (known as "Botalón") is accused of having committed 161 enforced disappearances, 108 forced displacements, 18 offenses of gender-based violence, and 355 illegal recruitments. He is also considered responsible for the massive displacement of farmers in the municipality of Quitaz, Belleza, Santander, in 2001.

Edward Cobos (commonly known as "Diego Vecino") is accused of having committed 108 enforced disappearances, 280 forced displacements, 30 offenses of gender-based violence, and 30 illegal recruitments. He has been sentenced to 39 years in prison for the massacre of Mampujan, 11 homicides, 17 kidnappings, and 1,081 cases of forced displacement.

Miguel Mejía Múnera (known as "El Mellizo") is accused of having committed 232 enforced disappearances, 568 forced displacements, 16 offenses of gender-based violence, and ten illegal recruitments. In addition, he is considered responsible for the murder of trade unionist leaders and two journalists in 2003.

Edgar Cifuentes (known as "El Aguila") is considered responsible for 33 enforced disappearances, 122 forced displacements, and six illegal recruitments.

Freddy Rendón (commonly known as "El Alemán") is accused of having committed 55 enforced disappearances, 914 forced displacements, 16 offenses of gender-based violence, and 12 illegal recruitments. He is also held responsible for the massacre of Horqueta, Cundinamarca, in 1997. He has been sentenced to 54 years in prison for homicide, kidnapping, and child recruitment.

Ever Veloza (commonly known as "HH") is accused of having committed 95 enforced disappearances, 941 forced displacements, 42 offenses of gender-based violence, and 40 illegal recruitments. He is also considered responsible for the massacre of "Saiza," which took place in the department of Córdoba in 1991.

Hernán Giraldo is considered responsible for 192 enforced disappearances, 2,210 forced displacements, 35 offenses of gender-based violence, and 56 illegal recruitments. He is also accused of murdering environmentalists and members of the indigenous movement.

Oscar José Ospino (commonly known as "Tolemaida") is accused of having committed 14 enforced disappearances, seven forced displacements, five offenses of gender-based violence, and seven illegal recruitments. He is also held responsible for more than 8,500 victims of the massacres in the municipalities of Bahía Portete, Nueva Valencia, and El Salado.

Iván Roberto Duque (known as "Ernesto Baéz") is held responsible for the massacre of Guadualito, which took place in the department of Putumayo in 1994. In addition, he is accused of having caused the displacement of Vallecito in the department of Bolivar in 2001, and of committing around 20 selective murders.

Uber Enrique Bánquez (commonly known as "Juancho Dique") is accused of having committed the massacre of Mampujan, murdering 11 people, conducting 17 kidnappings, and causing the displacement of 1,081 people. He has been sentenced to 39 years in prison.

Edgar Ignacio Fierro has been sentenced to 40 years in prison after being found guilty of 101 homicides, 12 enforced disappearances, 124 forced displacements, torture, and sexual abuse.

Rodrigo Tovar Pupo (commonly known as "Jorge 40") is accused of having committed 197 crimes, among which are aggravated murders, attempted aggravated murders, manufacturing and trafficking of weapons, kidnapping, enforced disappearances, homicides of protected persons, terrorism, and forced displacements. In addition, he is held responsible for the massacre of 26 people in Playón, Magdalena, on January 9, 1999, and for the murder of 11 people in Villanueva, La Guajira, on December 7, 1998. The crimes under investigation took place in La Guajira, Magdalena, Cesar, and Atlántico, where a network of paramilitary groups known as the Bloque Norte (North Block) was located.

Juan Carlos Sierra (commonly known as "El Tuso") is accused of criminal conspiracy, financing terrorism, the administration of resources related to terrorist activities, money laundering, the illegal possession of weapons, the illegal employment of communication devices, and drug trafficking.

Conclusions

Until now, the attempts made to explain these types of behaviors have not been fruitful. In the general study of terrorism, no scientific evidence has been found for the possibility of a mental illness preceding terrorist behavior and leading to these brutal acts. In this regard, Silke (2003) argues that terrorists are, in general, "normal" people. According to psychological theory, for example, there is a specific characteristic of terrorist group members that guides their extreme degree of participation in group processes. This extreme participation creates a bond between the members of the organization, which is effectively reinforced by the group leader to maximize their cohesion, solidarity, and self-confidence.

Canadian researcher Gustav Morf (1970) studied a group of terrorists who belonged to the Front de Libération du Québec (Quebec Liberation Front), but he did not observe a personality trait that could be considered characteristic of this population. In a similar way, Rash (as cited in Horgan, 2005), a German psychiatrist, undertook the study of 11 male and female members of the terrorist group Baader-Meinhof. He did not find signs of paranoia, psychopathy, neurological disturbances, or psychotic disorders. Contrary to what is suggested by McCauley

(2007), these findings do not necessarily mean that terrorists do not suffer from specific pathologies; instead, such pathologies might not have appeared at significantly different degrees from the control groups that were examined. Therefore, it has not been possible to conclude that terrorist group members generally have serious mental or personality disorders.

As noted by Horgan (2005), only a small group of psychologists has undertaken primary research with reliable data obtained from interviews with both terrorists and incarcerated or active criminals. In Colombia, however, no research has been conducted with paramilitary members and thus no possible explanation for their behavior can be determined from empirical data.

Many questions result from the observation of paramilitary atrocities. The fact that most paramilitary members and leaders do not come from poor or uneducated backgrounds and were not victims of violence in their past is a fact that does not cease to astound. By contrast, some of the most brutal paramilitary murderers are college graduates, members of prestigious families, political leaders, landowners, farmers, former State employees, military servicemen, and policemen.

There is no doubt that the extreme violence that has been exerted by paramilitarism in Colombia requires a broad and committed study approached from the social sciences. Such a study could allow an understanding to be gained of both the specific circumstances of terrorist and merciless acts and the social context in which these events take place. Today, more than ever, there is a need for systematic and committed research that considers the difficult and constant risks involved in studying the subject while also seeking to overcome such risks.

Notes

1 Fernando Díaz Colorado is a teacher in the Law and Psychology departments at several Colombian universities. He is also a teacher of criminology at the Humani Institute in Leon, Guanajuato, Mexico. He has spoken nationally and internationally on subjects related to victimology, criminology, and legal psychology.

2 "Los pájaros" were combatants of conservative ideology who fought against groups of liberal ideologies. These groups originated in the departments of Caldas and Boyacá, and then extended to Valle del Cauca during the 1940s. In the opinion of Betancourt and García (1990), "los pájaros" came together as one, a "dark and gloomy force" that "mobilized to intimidate, pressure and murder" and, after acting, "disappeared beneath a thick blanket of smoke tended by leading Conservatives, authorities and public officials" (p. 251).

3 "Chulavitas" was a name given to an armed group that existed during the mid-twentieth century in Colombia. Its combatants were from the Chulavita village in the municipality of Boabita, located in the department of Boyacá. They defended a conservative ideology and opposed the liberals or "cachiporros." They also committed massacres, murders, and crimes against different populations.

4 The friend–enemy distinction drawn up by Schmitt involves identifying with a substantive characteristic or ideology (us) that is in opposition to another (them). The us–them difference establishes a principle of opposition and complementarity, and the perception that a group develops of itself in relation to others is both a cohesive and distinguishing element. Recognizing the enemy involves identification with a political project that generates a sense of belonging (Mouffe, 1999).

5 In Colombia, the number of victims of the paramilitaries is not clear. These figures were provided by the General Prosecutor's Office of the investigations conducted and therefore are only part of the data.

References

Aranguren, M. (2002). *Mi Confesión: Carlos Castaño Revela Sus Secretos* [*My Confession: Carlos Castaño Reveals His Secrets*]. Bogotá, Colombia: Oveja Negra.

Arcieri, V. (2007). El desentierro de la verdad [Digging for the truth]. *El Tiempo*, August 8.

Betancourt, D., & García, M. (1990). *Matones y Cuadrilleros: Origen y Evolución de la Violencia en el Occidente Colombiano* [*Bullies and Cuadrilleros: Origin and Evolution of Violence in the Colombian West*]. Bogotá, Colombia: Tercer Mundo and Instituto de Estudios Políticos y Relaciones Internacionales Universidad Nacional de Colombia.

Blair, E. (2001). El espectáculo del dolor, el sufrimiento y la crueldad [The spectacle of truth, suffering and cruelty]. *Controversia*, 178(1), 82–99.

Campbell, B. (2000). *Death Squads: Definition, Problems and Historical Context*. New York, NY: St. Martin's Press.

Castro, M. (2002). Investiduras, destrozos y cicatrices o del cuerpo en la guerra [Investiture, wounds and scars of the body in war]. *Desde el Jardín de Freud Revista de Psicoanálisis*, 2(1), 38–45.

Centro Nacional de Memoria Histórica (2010). *!Basta Ya! Colombia: Memorias de Guerra y Dignidad* [*Enough! Colombia: Memories of War and Dignity*]. Bogotá, Colombia: Grupo de Memoria Histórica.

Colorado, A., Gaitán, P., Gonzales, F., Machado, A., Orozco, I., Restrepo, J., ... & Wills, E. (2008). *Trujillo: A Tragedy That Does Not Stop*. A report of the Historical Memory Commission. Bogotá, Colombia: Planeta.

Correa, C., & Rueda, D. (2002). La barbarie irracional de la guerra: El desplazamiento [The irrational barbarity of war: The displacement]. In: Bello, M., Cardinal, E., & Arias, F. (eds), *Efectos Psicosociales y Culturales del Desplazamiento* [*Psychosocial and Cultural Effects of Displacement*]. Bogotá, Colombia: Universidad Nacional de Colombia. pp. 64–77.

Corredor, C. (1990). Crisis agraria, reforma y paz: de la violencia homicida al genocidio [Agrarian crisis, reform and peace. From homicidal violence to genocide]. *Controversia*, 151–152(2), 19–78.

Cubides, F. (1999). *Los Paramilitares y Su Estrategia* [*The Paramilitaries and Their Strategy*]. Bogotá, Colombia: Uniandes.

Díaz, C.F. (2002). El secuestro: Aspectos éticos y práctica psicojurídica [Kidnapping: Ethical aspects and psycho-legal practice]. *Universitas*, 103(1), 125–127.

Dudley, S. (2008). *Armas y Urnas: Historia de un Genocidio Político* [*Arms and Urns: A History of a Political Genocide*]. Bogotá, Colombia: Temis.

Duque, L. (2009). Expresión simbólica de la práctica paramilitar, de violencia y destrucción del cuerpo de sus victimas, en el marco del conflicto armado Colombiano [Symbolic expression of paramilitary practices of violence and destruction of the victims' bodies in the context of the Colombian armed conflict] (Unpublished dissertation). Pontificia Universidad Javeriana, Bogotá.

Erickson, K. (1994). *A New Species of Trouble: The Human Experience of Modern Disasters*. New York, NY: Norton.

Gonzáles, C.P. (2011). *Consolidaciòn Territorial y Resurgimiento de Paras y Guerrilla* [*Territorial Consolidation and the Resurgence of Paras and Guerrillas*]. Bogotá, Colombia: INDEPAZ.

Guzmán, C., Fals, B., & Umaña, E. (1998). *La Violencia en Colombia* [*Violence in Colombia*]. Bogotá, Colombia: Círculo de Lectores.

Hoffman, B. (2003). The logic of suicide terrorism. *The Atlantic Monthly*, 291(5), 40–47.

Horgan, J. (2005). *Psicología del Terrorismo* [*Psychology of Terrorism*]. Barcelona, Spain: Gedisa.

Huggins, M. (1991). *Vigilantism and the State in the Modern Latin American: Essay on Extralegal Violence.* New York, NY: Praeger.

Human Rights Watch (2001). La sexta division: Relaciones militares–paramilitares y la política estadounidense en Colombia [The sixth division: Military–paramilitary relations and American politics in Colombia]. Retrieved on February 11, 2016 from: www.hrw.org/legacy/spanish/informes/2001/sexta_division2.html.

Ignatieff, M. (1999). Los rencorosos que esperaron para matar [The resentful who waited to kill]. In: Wimmer, A., Goldstone, R., Horowitz, D., Joras, U., & Schetter, C. (eds), *Facing Ethnic Conflicts.* New York, NY: Rowman & Littlefield.

Manitzas, H. (1991). *All the Minister's Men: Paramilitary Activity in Peru.* New York, NY: Praeger.

Maya, M. (2012). Las cuentas no son tan alegres [The accounts are not that good]. February 10–16, 2012. Retrieved on January 5, 2017 from: http://viva.org.co/cajavirtual/svc0290/articulo06.html.

McCauley, C. (2007). *Psychological Issues in Understanding Terrorism and the Response to Terrorism.* Wesport, CT: Greenwood Publishing.

Morf, G. (1970). *Terror in Quebec: Case Studies of the FLQ.* Toronto, Canada: Clark Irwing.

Mouffe, C. (1999). *El Retorno de lo Político: Comunidad, Ciudadania, Pluralism, Democracia Radical* [*The Return of the Political: Community, Citizenship, Pluralism, Radical Democracy*]. Barcelona, Spain: Paidós Iberica.

PAX (2014). *The Dark Side of Coal: Paramilitary Violence in the Cesar Region, Colombia.* Bogotá, Colombia: Christian Organization PAX.

Pinto, B. (1989). Las masacres, desinformación y violencia [Massacres, disinformation and violence], *Revista Trocadero*, 4(6), 3–7.

Rangel, A. (2007). *El Poder Paramilitary* [*Paramilitary Power*]. Bogotá, Colombia: Planeta.

Rementería, I. (2009). La guerra de las drogas: Cien años de crueldad y fracasos sanitarios [The drug war: One hundred years of cruelty and health failures]. *Nueva Sociedad*, 222(1), 70–80.

Revista Semana (1990). Rambo. *Revista Semana*, May 21. Retrieved on January 5, 2017 from: www.semana.com/nacion/articulo/rambo/13331-3.

Revista Semana (2007a). Canibalismo paramilitar [Paramilitary cannibalism]. *Revista Semana*, August 4. Retrieved on January 5, 2017 from: www.semana.com/enfoque/articulo/canibalismo-paramilitar/87423-3.

Revista Semana (2007b). Informe especial: La Barbarie que no vimos los Colombianos [Special report: The barbarity that we Colombians did not see]. *Revista Semana*, August 8. Retrieved on January 5, 2017 from: www.ddhh-colombia.org/html/noticias%20ddhh/labarbariequenovimosdciembre82007.pdf.

Robin, K. (2003). *Más Terible que la Muerte: Masacres, Drogas y la Guerra de Estados Unidos en Colombia* [*More Terrible than Death: Massacres, Drugs and America's War in Colombia*]. Barcelona, Spain: Paidos Iberica.

Ronderos, M.T. (2014). *Guerras Recicladas* [*Recycled Wars*]. Bogotá, Colombia: Aguilar.

Silke, A. (2003). Deindividuation, anonymity and violence: Findings from Northern Ireland. *Journal of Social Psychology*, 143(4), 493–509.

Suarez, C., & Martínez, M. (2009). El estudio de la violencia más allá del espectáculo de la sangre. *Universitas Humanística*, 67(1), 13–28.

Torres, A. (2006). Paramiliatres coombianos confoersan como descuartizaban a sus víctimas [Paramilitary soldiers confess how they dismembered victims]. *El Tiempo*, April 24.

Uribe, M.V. (1990). Matar, rematar y contramatar: Las masacres en el Tolima 1948–1964 [Kill and kill again: Massacres in the Tolima 1948–1964]. *Controversia* 159–160(1).

Uribe, M.V. (2004). *Antropología de la Inhumanidad [Anthropology of Inhumanity]*. Bogotá, Colombia: Norma.

Uribe, M., & Vásquez, T. (1995). *Enterrar y Callar: Las Masacres en Colombia, 1980–1993 [Bury and Shut: Massacres in Colombia, 1980–1993]*. Bogotá, Colombia: Comité Permanente por la Defensa de los Derechos Humanos.

Velásquez, E. (2007). La historia del paramilitarismo en Colombia [The history of paramilitarism in Colombia]. *História, Sao Paulo*, 26(1), 134–153.

Warren, K. (1998). *Indigenous Movements and Their Critics: Pan Maya Activism in Guatemala.* Princeton, NJ: Princeton University Press.

Wieviorka, M. (1991). *El Terrorismo: La Violencia Política en el Mundo [Terrorism: Political Violence in the World]*. Madrid, Spain: Plaza y Janes.

10

CONCLUSIONS

Introduction

Morality can be considered a series of principles or ideals that help an individual to distinguish between good and evil and to act in life according to this distinction. These principles guide and rule social interaction and, without them, society would be chaotic. It is often considered that human morality has several components (Myyry, 2003; Rest, 1984), which are:

- *emotional component:* feelings associated with thought and moral behavior, such as guilt, shame, or pride;
- *cognitive component:* the manner in which we think about a moral problem and in which we take decisions about what is right and what is wrong;
- *behavioral component:* how we behave, including the degree to which we can lie, cheat, or behave with honor.

A healthy and honest personality is associated with congruence between these three components. When one of them does not exist, conflicts arise; for example, we can know at a cognitive level that cheating is wrong, but at a behavioral level we may continue to cheat (i.e. there is a deficiency in the behavioral component). In the same way, some people have lives that could be considered very good, but they feel guilt most of the time (i.e. there is a deficiency in the emotional component).

We as human beings are endowed with a benign aggression that drives us to act in an assertive way when we feel that we have been deprived of something valuable to which we believe we have the right. In addition, we need to feel that our behavior is justified, that we are valued, and that we are important to someone. Part of our fascination with and attraction to the cases of violent criminals and serial killers emerges from the fact that their minds seem to not be different from ours. However, they are different from us in that they display extreme aspects of the human being. Because of this, we ask ourselves: what is the difference between one person and another who is able to commit homicides, abuse children or old people, or humiliate relatives and employees?

The ability of violent criminals to describe the most atrocious crimes with an overwhelming coldness is astounding. A common factor among all of them is that they possess a cognitive system that allows them to filter reality to validate their desire to cause harm. It is common that self-exonerating and self-justifying thoughts allow them to break social rules and eliminate all traces of guilt or anxiety. In all violent criminals, there is a contradiction between the cognitive understanding of the illegality of their behavior and the emotional meaning of this illegality.

Likewise, in our experience, all of the criminals with whom we have maintained contact are aware that there are social and legal rules that forbid what they are doing, but, at the same time, they are convinced that their actions are in some way justified. They also often believe that they are victims, not victimizers. Such people in fact have moral values that allow them to determine what is an appropriate behavior and what is not, but they do not apply them to themselves in the same way. It is common for them to blame other people for their actions. For example, one of the killers whom we had the chance to interview, who had killed and dismembered his lover, said that he did not feel any remorse because the only person responsible for what had happened was his lover, because she deceived him, telling him she had left her husband. In other words, in their minds, many criminals perceive themselves as victims who punish those people who deserve it.

We must bear in mind that criminality can be associated with biological predispositions—including genetic predispositions—to commit impulsive and violent acts and the interactions of such predispositions with psychological and social factors. For example, our degree of impulsivity depends on the level of a brain neurotransmitter known as serotonin, whose levels can decrease through alcohol consumption. Likewise, our degree of aggressiveness depends on the quantity of testosterone, which can increase with steroids. Scientific studies have proved that brain malfunctions that alter the level of these chemical substances in the brain are the cause of an inability to inhibit violent impulses (Nelson & Chiavegatto, 2001). Therefore, in this field, it is not strange to find that neurological alterations lead many killers to become victims of their impulses. It needs to be made clear that this damage is not necessarily structural, but it can also be functional.

It is paradoxical that, while there are a lot of people who personify things, such as by giving names—and even attributing emotions—to their favorite objects, criminals treat people as objects, which allows them to torture and kill them without experiencing any remorse or guilt. By not emotionally identifying themselves with the victims, nothing prevents them from justifying their actions.

It is important to emphasize that many criminals have a history of inadequate socialization (Hare & Neumann, 2009). One of the most important factors in the life of a child is the attachment to his or her parents. Domestic violence, either through abuse from a partner or maltreatment during childhood, interferes with the formation of a strong and positive bond. That is to say, by being exposed to domestic violence or rejection, a child's emotions are clouded and his or her ability to form attachments is reduced. The development of an insecure bond between a child and his or her caregiver predisposes the person to aggression (Tremblay, 2003).

All this leads us to consider that criminality is not necessarily associated with a lack of material resources and poverty, but is a phenomenon that often emerges within dysfunctional families. It is very common to find that criminals have experienced a lack of paternal attention and that the relationship they had with their mother was marked by coldness, distance, abandonment, and a lack of emotional warmth or physical contact. These kinds of infants are sometimes deeply mistreated and often live as hurt children in the bodies of adults. Once they are imprisoned, they are prone to worshipping religious figures to relieve their anguish, depression, and loneliness and perhaps to find their lost or non-existent bonds.

Educate to Coexist

One of the main conclusions of this book is the importance of distinguishing between primary and secondary violence. We talk about the latter when it is the result of external conditions. Some people display violent behaviors as a result of factors such as depression, substance and alcohol abuse, trauma to the head, and psychiatric disorders (e.g. schizophrenia, paranoid disorders), or as a result of personality disorders such as borderline personality disorder. In addition, several environmental factors can worsen violence, such as sleep deprivation, the use of stimulants, excessive heat, and daily frustrations. We also note the existence of primary aggression—that is, aggression in a violent individual that is not linked to the aforementioned factors.

Understanding the relationship between violence and the factors that precipitate it can help in its prevention and treatment. The basic premise from which we can start is that, in the case of secondary violence, it is important to treat the principal cause to be able to control it.

Primary violence is displayed in two ways: impulsive or premeditated. This distinction is important, because these two forms of violence differ in several ways: the events that trigger or provoke them, the reactions that are displayed, the related brain activity, and the possible medical and psychological treatments. Despite the fact that the biological aspects underlying violent behavior, including antisocial personality, psychopathy, borderline personality, and other types of aggressive personalities, have occasionally been emphasized, it is important to note that violent behavior is generally not solely caused by these disorders, but is the result of interactions between a variety of psychological, biological, and social variables.

Experiencing physical and psychological abuse during childhood, psychiatric disorders that lead to a paranoid and suspicious attitude, and the presence of brain dysfunction and/or damage are important causal factors in the generation and development of violence. Each one of these variables increases the probability of an individual becoming aggressive, but when the three factors are combined, the possibility of a violent personality emerging becomes very high.

How can we reduce violence? The importance of these scientific discoveries is that, if society is able to prevent one of these factors, the possibility of violent personalities developing will be greatly reduced.

In relation to social factors, it is necessary to mention that a large part of the antisocial behavior that individuals with premeditated aggression display is of an instrumental nature; that is, the objective is to take others' money or to gain sexual favors, respect, or control. In general, such individuals try to achieve these goals through diverse means. Undoubtedly, a person of a high socio-economic level has more alternative options available to them to achieve some of these objectives than an individual of a low socio-economic level. There is an association between sociocultural level, biological factors, socialization, and antisocial personality, but low sociocultural level limits a person's behavioral options. For example, if a man has 100,000 Mexican pesos, the subjective value he puts on stealing 50 pesos from another person in the street is very low. By contrast, if he has only 50 cents, the subjective value he places on 50 Mexican pesos is very high. However, we know that an individual of a low socio-economic level who has a healthy biological system and appropriate socialization patterns acquired during upbringing will not resort to antisocial behaviors to achieve his or her goals, whatever his or her needs.

How can we educate children to display honesty and self-control in a complex and morally ambiguous world, where traditional bonds between the family, school, and the community are unstable? All children are born with the potential and drive for moral development. A number of innate factors predispose them to act in an ethical way. For example, empathy is part of human nature: newborns cry when they hear other babies crying and show signs of pleasure when they hear sounds of happiness, such as laughing. However, despite having this innate emotional disposition, how to effectively help other people must be learned and refined through social experience.

To become people with moral principles, children need to not only learn to distinguish between what is right and what is wrong, but also develop moral integrity so that they present themselves and act in line with this. Moral development is a gradual process in which consistency must exist between the information that a child receives from his or her parents and school, the media, and the community.

Educating children to be committed to the values of honesty, self-discipline, and compromise requires much more than theoretical lessons about values. Moral education requires explicit instruction, exhortation, and training. We have to involve children in the problems, use debates with classmates, and engage support from the community and parents. Ethics must be linked to actions in the community.

Philosophical Implications: Violence, Free Will, and Laws

Thanks to advances in scientific methods applied to the study of violent and psychopathic individuals, the biological bases and brain mechanisms that underlie these behaviors have been partially identified—factors that can affect the survival of the social group.

Neuropsychological, electrophysiological, and neuroimaging techniques are revolutionizing our understanding of the brain structures that are involved in emotions and in decision making. However, their use and interpretation also have ethical problems, since the results could be used in the case of criminals as an argument to reduce their degree of responsibility and therefore to help them to avoid significant sentences or imprisonment.

Within the philosophical field, as Adrian Raine points out, the issue of the existence of free will in these people is raised (Raine, 2008; Raine & Yang, 2006). Are their criminal acts a result of their freedom of choice and under their control? Are these individuals able to choose between assaulting and not assaulting someone? According to Raine, if we imagine free will as a straight line between two points, at one point we would have people who almost completely control their actions (the maximum expression of free will) and at the other point are those people who do not control their actions at all. Even though nowadays science is not a threat to free will, our acquired knowledge delimits the space in which free will can operate. Under this assumption, it could be speculated that it is possible to demarcate the mechanisms that are involved in decision making. There are a series of social, biological, and genetic mechanisms that have a decisive role in the configuration of free will, and only through serious and committed studies will we be able to provide appropriate justice when dealing with those individuals who are limited by brain alterations that reduce their control.

There is still plenty of work required in understanding and treating violence and its disorders. However, there is hope that, through science, a progressive solution to this serious problem could be found. Although there are currently no effective treatments for psychopathy, progress is being made in the development of cognitive skills with training programs that are directed to promote a psychopath's empathy (Wong & Hare, 2005). These therapies draw from the belief that a psychopath's behavior emerges from a serious inability to process emotions.

Even though a psychopath does not suffer from a "mental disorder" in the legal sense of the term, he or she is legally treated in a different way from a person who does not suffer from any illness. Therefore, he or she cannot be exempted because of illness, sentencing is different, and the choice of whether he or she receives therapy is not up to him or her. The goal we must pursue is to help such people to develop a real comprehension of other people's thoughts and feelings, to broaden their vision of the world, and to create new interpretations of social norms and obligations. Only through serious and committed studies will we someday be able to thoroughly comprehend and prevent the phenomenon of violence.

References

Hare, R.D., & Neumann, C.S. (2009). *Psychopathy*. New York, NY: Oxford University Press.

Myyry, L. (2003). *Components of Morality*. Helsinki, Finland: University of Helsinki.

Nelson, R.J., & Chiavegatto, S. (2001). Molecular basis of aggression. *Trends in Neurosciences*, 24(12), 713–719.

Raine, A. (2008). From genes to brain to antisocial behavior. *Current Directions in Psychological Science*, 17(5), 323–328.

Raine, A., & Yang, Y. (2006). The neuroanatomical bases of psychopathy. In: Patrick, C.J. (ed.), *Handbook of Psychopathy*. New York, NY: Guilford Press. pp. 278–295.

Rest, J.R. (1984). The major components of morality. In: Kurtines, W.M., & Gewirtz, J.L. (eds), *Morality, Moral Behavior, and Moral Development*. New York, NY: Wiley. pp. 24–38.

Tremblay, R.E. (2003). *Why Socialization Fails: The Case of Chronic Physical Aggression*. New York, NY: Guilford Press.

Wong, S.C., & Hare, R.D. (2005). *Guidelines for a Psychopathy Treatment Program*. Toronto, Canada: Multi-Health Systems.

INDEX